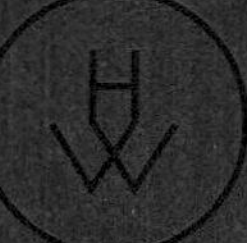

LYGIA PAPE

Hauser & Wirth Publishers

With thanks to Paula Pape, Ricardo Fortes,
and the entire Projeto Lygia Pape

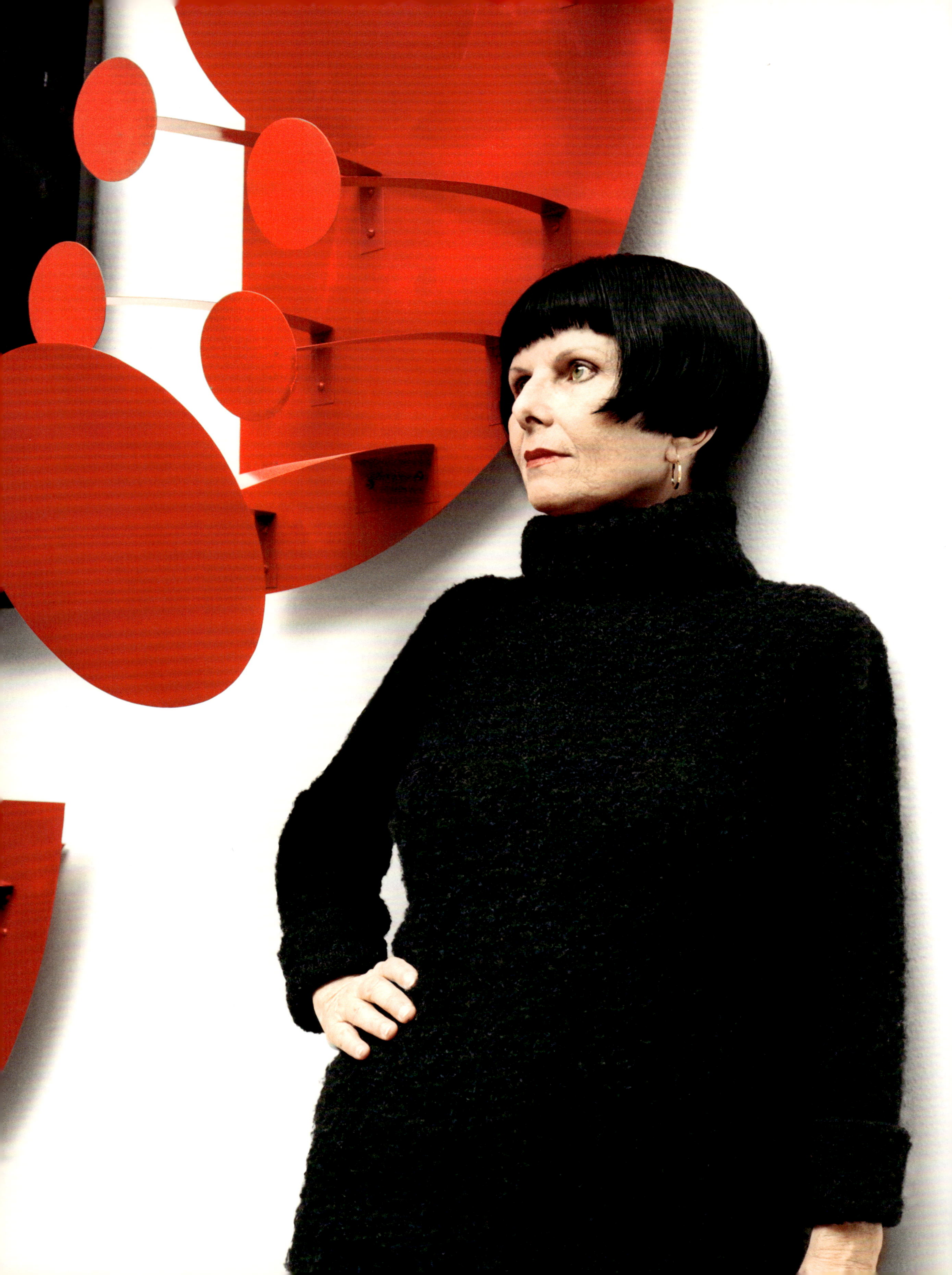

TEXTS

PLATES

"Like the Skin of a Whale":
The Pluri-sensorial Art of Lygia Pape

Alexander Alberro

When sometime around 1950 Lygia Pape began to identify as a visual artist, she was quickly caught up in the fascination with geometric abstraction that had recently gripped the most ambitious elements of Brazil's art scene. But over the course of her long career, Pape's investigation of space and perception was to bring her to an art that was focused not on optical but on haptic visuality, expressed in pluri-sensorial works that mobilize and appeal to the spectator's participatory and embodied experience.

The concrete art of the Argentinian Asociación de Arte Concreto-Invención, which featured the work of Tomás Maldonado, Lidy Prati, and others, had recently been exhibited in several Brazilian locations; in 1950 Swiss artist Max Bill's retrospective at the Museu de Arte de São Paulo was receiving an enthusiastic reception; and São Paulo-based artists Waldemar Cordeiro, Luiz Sacilotto, and Lothar Charoux were well into the discussions that would lead to the formation of the Grupo Ruptura, which championed concrete art's method of production.[1] Décio Vieira and many of the artists who Pape befriended while living in Petrópolis in 1951 were awed by concrete art's geometric vocabulary, as well as by the clarity and order it made evident.

Concrete art would reverberate quite extensively throughout Brazil during that decade.

The painter Ivan Serpa, to whom Vieira introduced Pape when she moved to Rio de Janeiro in 1952, and who would remain an important interlocutor of hers for many years to come, was at the time developing work that took up those aspects of concrete art that concern perceptual investigation.[2] These are related to the gestalt tendencies that Serpa and his associates—including artists Almir Mavignier and Abraham Palatnik, and the critic Mário Pedrosa, who had written a doctoral thesis on gestalt—saw in concrete art: the image on the plastic form is a fully anticipated one, a proto-image accessible at a glance, and above, or at least outside of, the realm of sense experience. Art, from this perspective, was a means of communicating knowledge that, though plainly visible, had hitherto been inaccessible. Although it denied all forms of naturalism, the central task of concrete art was the elucidation of actual phenomena. This led directly to an interest in mathematics and physics as the basis for understanding how art stimulates the human senses. It made perception quantifiable. Yet, what is perceived is conditioned by a whole layer of what itself seems to escape perception:

the rationalism that codifies the cultural techniques involved in the production of the artwork.

By the time she began to meet informally with Vieira, Aluísio Carvão, João José da Silva Costa, and other artists, first at Serpa's residence and then at the Ministry of Education and Health building where he taught art classes in 1953, Pape was making medium-scale (seventy-by-one-hundred centimeter) oil paintings on canvas.[3] These were quasi-geometrical, friezelike works with simple, pared-down forms in pale colors and black. Concrete art, especially the variant of it that became dominant in Brazil in the early 1950s, maintained that both expression and figuration were obsolete, and that only by streamlining form and arriving at an art of clarity, stability, and order could the crisis of belief that confronted the visual arts at this historical juncture be resolved. Canvases had to be understood only as planes, as defined spaces, and compositions as experiments of interdependencies. Parallel to Serpa, Carvão, and da Silva Costa, Pape—who was essentially self-taught in the fine arts—initially adopted these concerns. But she appears to have been unwilling to follow the general a priori axioms that concrete art in Brazil came to require. While she rejected all forms of

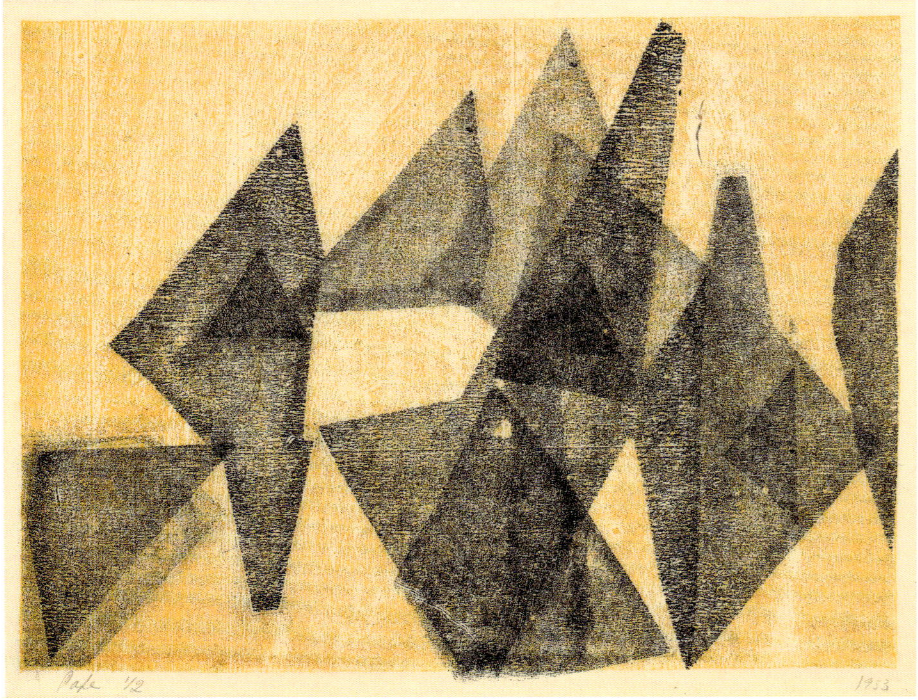

—fig. 1 *Tecelar*, 1953

non-figuration that sought the mere excitement of pleasure and displeasure, her early production also stayed clear of concrete art's strict demand that artworks function as a means of conceptually deducible knowledge.

EARLY WOODCUT ENGRAVINGS

Pape strayed even further from the schematic, abstract designs of concrete art when she began to produce constructive woodcut prints, initially conceived of as unique objects. These typically featured some geometric but mostly irregular elements floating in space. There are rotating rectangles, shifting rhomboids, triangles, and ovals of different opacity. A case in point is *Tecelar*, 1953 (fig. 1), which is made up of several geometric forms, mostly triangular, overlaid on one another.[4] Despite the simplicity of the shapes and patterns, the composition is complex, giving the semblance of intersection, tessellation, and superimposition, made subtler by the uneven application of ink on the template, with some areas bolder than others, which gives the forms a spectral quality. The overlaps and the organic vocabulary of these meditative abstractions make it difficult to distinguish foreground from background and soften the

effects of the individual elements. Pape found that if instead of a single plank she used separate printing blocks of distinct kinds of porous and coursed wood, she could break up the integral pattern that the grain of the wood would otherwise generate and circumvent printmaking's traditional reproductive capacities. She became fascinated by the characteristic texture and veining of different types of wood, and the varying qualities and effects that could be obtained by sawing and sanding the streaked surface of the blocks, working against the striated wood with her engraving tool before making the print.[5]

Pape experimented as well with the thickness of the blade cuts, the bored lines, and the paper itself, which was usually thin but sometimes semitransparent. Occasionally, she used the separate blocks to apply a range of colored inks, which included subtle reds, greens, blues, and orange-golds. *Tecelar*, c. 1955 (fig. 2), for example, which consists of a rectangular sheet of Japanese rice paper in a portrait format, features a cutout plane with very light ink that bisects the composition vertically, taking up almost the entire right-hand side of the white field, and cuts the other side in half down the center with a horizontal jut that extends to

the framing edge. Above and below this projection on the left are heavily striated, black printed forms that are the result of the template having been carved flat. A trembling red line superimposed onto the lightly inked plane runs vertically down the right of the composition. The roughly hewn forms thus float within the rectangle in a somewhat organic manner, though they are also interlocked in an idiosyncratic spatial relationship that betrays a trace of geometry.

Unlike oil painting, the technique of woodcut production unfolds in not one but two phases—three, if Pape's practice of always drawing the pattern beforehand is taken into account. Once the design has been determined, the engraver physically cuts into the template with a burin, carving out lines and forms. This tactile process is followed by that of spreading the viscous ink on the wooden block, and then pressing the block onto paper, bearing down on the delicate white surface as one might with a seal or stamp. The sound of Pape maneuvering the roller as she applied industrial-grade pigment to the template, and then the haptic weight, restraint, and pulsation of the printing blocks on the skin of the paper, can almost be seen in her engravings, which de-sublimate image making, endowing

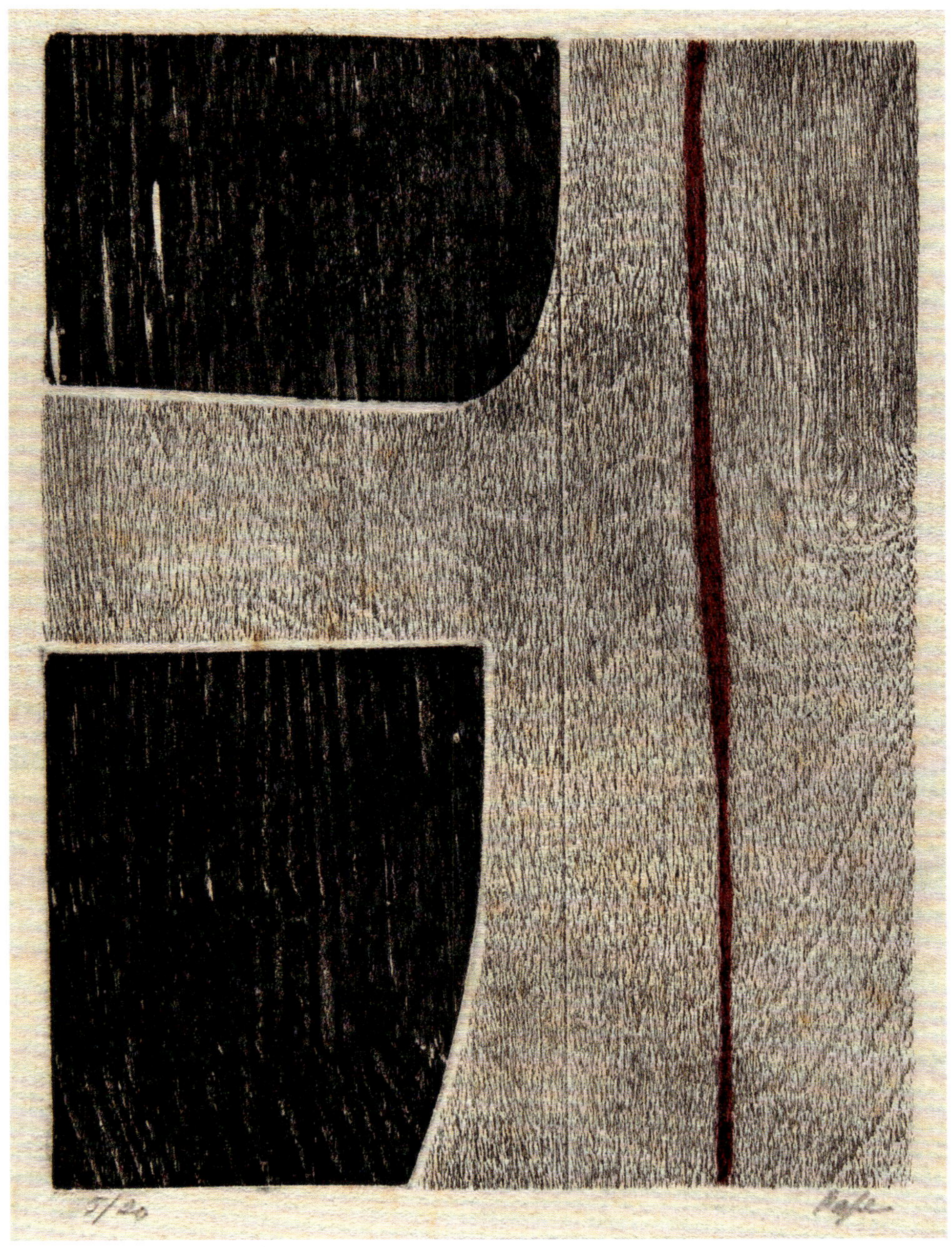

—fig. 2 *Tecelar*, c. 1955

it with a latent record of labor. Those physical, aural, and temporal aspects of the grinding production of the woodblock prints appeal to an embodied knowledge. They carry a material charge that takes the form of a kind of image-residue, an after-effect that tends to move over the surface and discern texture rather than distinguish form.[6]

Pape made a point to work with the surface—"with the grain of the wood," as she explained—and "to let the material, independent, expressive, speak for itself."[7] She sawed and sanded and physically bored into the organic matter that comprised the wooden blocks. One can speculate how the hours spent inches away from the templates and printing surfaces might have stimulated her sense of a close-up and tangible way of fashioning. The play that one can discern in her work between the natural veins and pores of the wood and the carving of the lines calls on the eye to linger over the innumerable surface effects; it generates prints that incorporate organic features and material sensoriality, and resemble what curator Paulo Herkenhoff once referred to as "scars on a skin that has a history of its own."[8]

GRUPO FRENTE

Pape's tenuous relationship to the aesthetics of concrete art shifted in 1954 as she, Serpa, and others founded what they referred to as "Grupo Frente," and held their first exhibition at the Galeria IBEU (Instituto Brasil-Estados Unidos) in Rio de Janeiro.[9] That same year she encountered the master engraver Fayga Ostrower, a war refugee whose family had emigrated from Poland to Brazil in the 1930s. Pape attended a few of the classes that Ostrower taught at the Museu de Arte Moderna in Rio de Janeiro (MAM-RJ), and picked up on the correspondence the latter articulated between technique and order as she explored the potential of engraving to materialize ideas.[10] "Mastery of technique enables better presentation of the idea and inventive richness," Pape wrote in a 1959 statement on printmaking, adding that by "inventive richness" she did "not mean the use of an infinite range of variations within the same work, but restrained solutions that are rigorous in their simplicity, and a formal–technical synthesis."[11]

Whether due to the classes with Ostrower, to discussions within Grupo Frente, or perhaps to something else altogether, Pape's woodcut engravings changed significantly in the mid-1950s. Pape limited her production materials to black ink, white paper, and single planks of overly grained wood. Her prints retained their nonrepresentational forms, but these now became increasingly analytical. Triangles and rectangular bands predominate in compositions that image a systematic repetition of rotationally symmetrical, geometric patterns on a flat surface. Their increased mathematical rigor was simultaneously reinforced and countered by the slight irregularities of the wood's coarse grain. This culminated in prints with a meticulously calculated coordination of pictorial elements across the surface plane in which the figure and ground appear woven together into cohesive, yet fractured, compositions. Special attention was paid to the nexus between positive and negative space. Masses and voids came to have similar value. Works such as *Tecelar* (fig. 3) and *Tecelar* (ill. p. 43), both 1955, feature polygons, trapezoids, parallelograms, and repeated stepped lines on a white background. Distinctions between top and bottom have been eliminated, as has color.

Pape also began to experiment with double printing to form a template, and the geometrical shapes delineated by black stripes and triangles in her engravings came to replicate each other and invert the

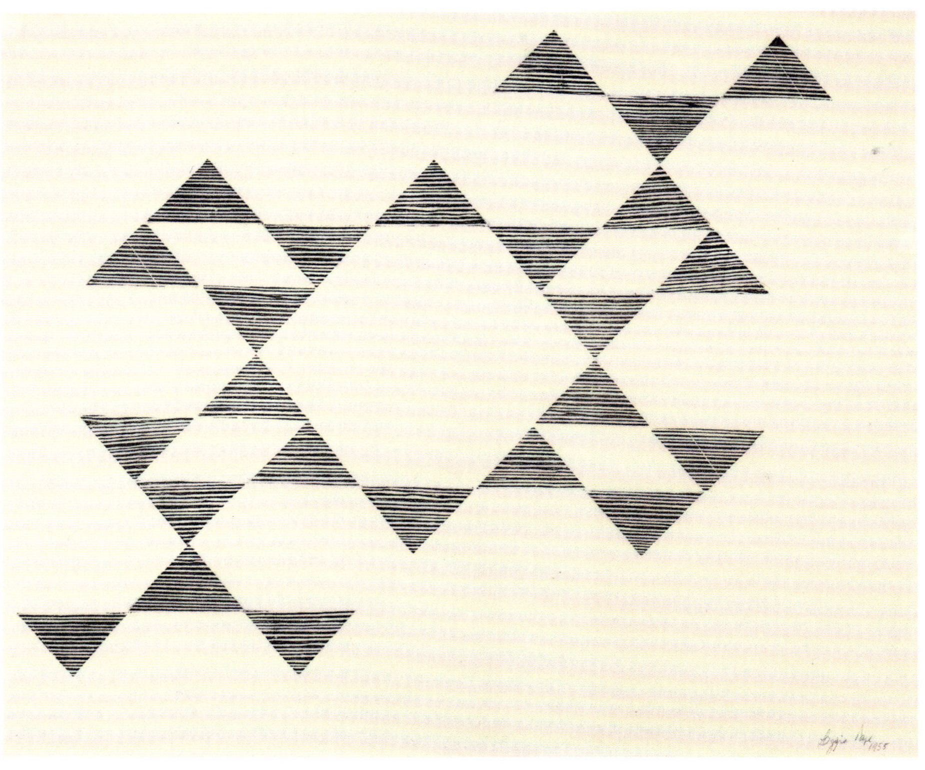

—fig. 3 *Tecelar*, 1955

composition across a central axis or by a dynamic diagonal encounter. The contrast between figure and ground begins to fluctuate in these prints, with their star-like patterns tilting as if to a rhythm. The spatial relationships between the component parts and the negative space is primary, the pictorial elements structured carefully across the plane, activating the surfaces.

Pape participated in two important national exhibitions—at the Museu de Arte Moderna in São Paulo (MAM-SP) in 1956, and at the Education and Cultural Ministry in Rio de Janeiro in 1957—events that demonstrated the productive mediation of concrete art in Brazil. She travelled with her husband to Europe in 1957, making a stop at the Ulm School of Design (Hochschule für Gestaltung Ulm) to visit Tómas Maldonado, the School's Rector, with whom she had taken a course at MAM-RJ in 1956, and to meet graphic designer Otl Aicher, with whom she would study, again at MAM-RJ, the following year. She also seems to have encountered the work of artist Josef Albers at around this time.

Art historian Sergio Martins notes that Albers figured prominently in the 1957 Bienal de São Paulo, and argues that "it is to [the work of Albers] that we must first turn in order to appreciate Pape's unique development of concretist woodcutting."[12] Indeed, Martins points out that critic Ferreira Gullar comments on correspondence between Albers and Pape in one of his short notices for the *Suplemento Dominical do Jornal do Brasil* (*SDJB*) in November 1957.[13] Albers was a master printmaker, and several of his series of the 1940s and 1950s featured geometrical designs in thin white lines carved into highly textured pinewood printing blocks. Similarities between the prints of Albers and Pape are evident. Yet, the differences are also highly revealing. Pape's engravings are much more wide-ranging in design than those of Albers, whose production in this medium was fairly consistent in style. Furthermore, as art historian Briony Fer has explained, whereas Albers "suspended his geometric configurations at the very center of each print, Pape preferred to extend hers right to the edge, where they seem to be cut out of, or unfolded from, larger structures still."[14] This distinction is important to make, for it brings to light two very different models of vision, one optical and the other haptic.

The optical visuality manifest in Albers's prints sees the designs represented from enough distance to perceive them as distinct forms in deep space: in other words, how vision is usually conceived, dependent upon a separation between the viewing subject and the object. The haptic manner of looking characteristically provoked by Pape's prints tends to move over the surface of the engraving rather than to plunge into illusionistic depth. This visuality seems more concerned with discerning texture than with distinguishing form; more inclined to peruse than to focus. Pape's engravings invite a glance that moves over the surface plane for some time before the spectator realizes what she or he is beholding. They resolve into figuration only gradually, if at all. In short, while Albers's prints privilege the representational power of the design, Pape's highlight the material presence of the engraving. They draw from forms of sense experience, such as that of touch, that exceed optical visuality. And insofar as touch is a sense located on the surface of the body, thinking of Pape's prints as haptic opens the way to considering the ways her work appeals to the body as a whole.

BLACK PRINTS

Pape followed the woodcut engravings of triangular and rectangular bands with black-ground works that

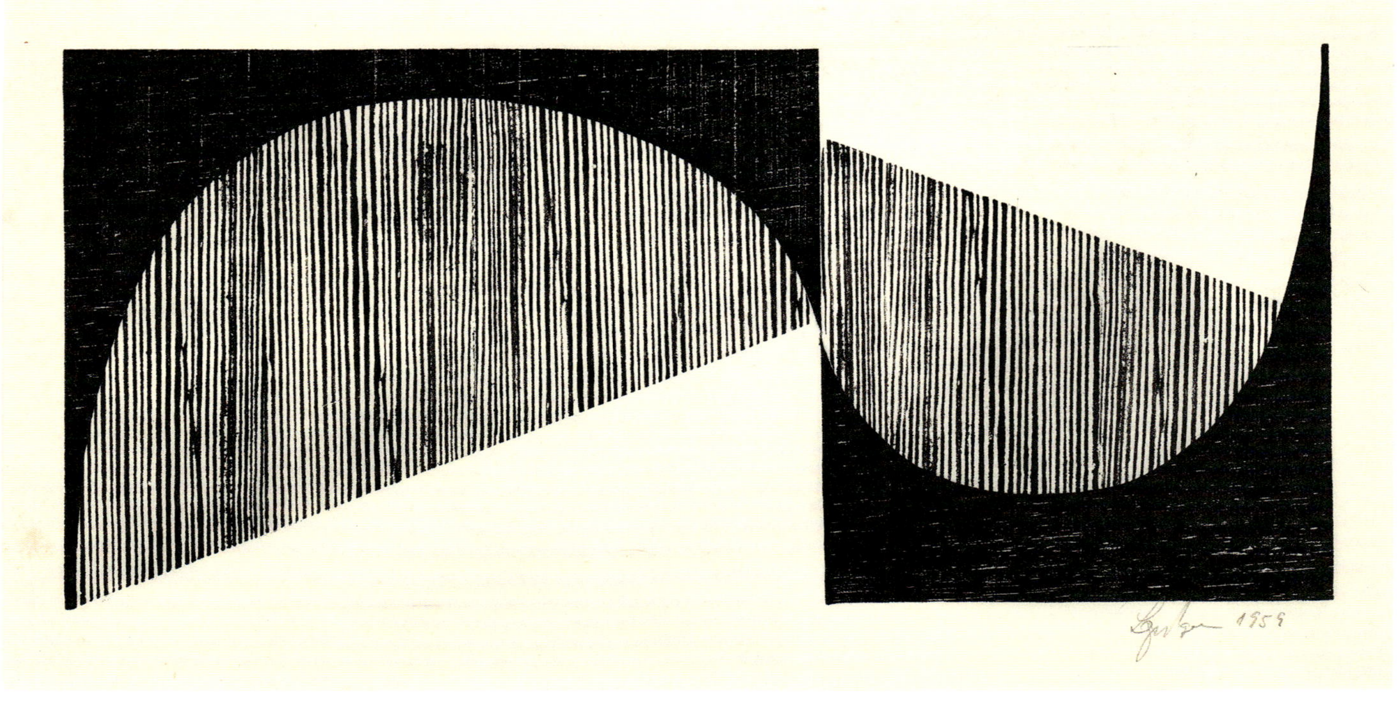

—fig. 4 *Tecelar*, 1959

feature a dense, dark, printed area inflected by a smooth, subtle wood grain and precisely cut parallel lines. (See *Tecelares*, ills. pp. 45 and 47, both 1958; also fig. 4 and ill. p. 46, both 1959.) This development was largely made possible by the artist's discovery that the more open the pores of the woodblock, the darker the black that could be achieved when inked and pressed onto thin Japanese rice paper. The abstract images with black backgrounds and designs that resulted from Pape's experiments with different types of wood, of varying porosity, feature geometric sequences of white parallel lines that blur the distinctness of the dark plane, causing the visual opposition of flat surfaces to dismantle. The printing plate in turn becomes the primary presence of the engraving, with the prints activating space through accumulations, overlappings, modulations, geometric inversions, and cuts. As Pape noted in retrospect when describing these artworks, the black of the templates now functioned as "printed color—surface—virtual space," while the white of the lines operated as "light—real space."[15] Within this dramatic use of black and white, the multiplication and profusion of lines came to be envisaged as light cast onto the blind and pitch-black surface of

the untouched woodblock, thereby opening up space within the plane.

The internal division of many of Pape's engravings is structured by a carved line that holds the formal elements of the composition together. The mark is at once a cut, a seam, and an opening to the surrounding space. Spatial tension and notions of aesthetic closure (the completeness of fixed, immutable art objects) are thereby eliminated in favor of privileging the material presence of the artwork, expanding the plane across different modalities and dimensions of space. This invites a more palpable kind of vision in which the sense of space is contingent, intimate, and full of possibility. The prints with their black surfaces and striated patterns of white lines appear to *breathe*, "like the skin of a whale," as Pape once phrased it, and put pressure on the distinction between virtual and real space.[16] Like crevices in the global topography, each of the prints comes forth as a locus of lines and actions. The grooves carved into the sanded-down surfaces of the woodblocks, coated in tacky black ink, generate a light that cuts sharply through the primal darkness. These lines of light illuminate a smooth space that "overflows the pictorial limit," as Pape's friend Hélio Oiticica put it when describing these 1950s engravings.[17]

NEOCONCRETE ART

Pape identified her later prints as neoconcrete. One was prominently illustrated in the "Neoconcrete Manifesto," written by Gullar and published in the *SDJB* in March 1959, on the day the first neoconcrete exhibition opened. The manifesto, which Pape—along with Amilcar de Castro, Franz Weissmann, Lygia Clark, Reynaldo Jardim, Theon Spanudis, and Gullar—signed, was accompanied in the same journal by a statement she penned on printmaking that in retrospect reads as a culmination of her work in the medium. (She would soon discontinue woodcut engraving altogether.) Titled "Gravura: Depoimento de Lygia Pape" (On Printmaking: A Statement by Lygia Pape), the text has Pape reflecting on six years of production; she presents herself as a master of the medium, and stresses that it is but one of several in which she works.[18] Pape reveals that she always draws the design before beginning to cut into the printing block, and considers the importance of "the characteristic texture and veining of each type of wood, . . . the thickness of the cuts, the lines, the paper itself." She explains: "The process of printmaking has a life of its own, before, during[,] and after the engraving is made." And yet, Pape emphasizes that "mastery of technique," while enabling a better presentation of the underlying idea, is itself insufficient. What is crucial is creativity, and especially the type of inventive richness that comes not by chance but sensorially, through "intuition." This leads her to identify the kind of printmaking that characterizes her practice—in which a vital and organic relationship between positive and negative space stretches the boundaries of the medium, generating an expanded space that breaks the formal tensions—as neoconcrete. Key to this expansion of space beyond the literal into the virtual realm are the white lines she cuts in the woodblocks:

> White lines crossing surfaces create virtual planes and give the measure of different times of these space–planes. . . . Those constructed in two dimensions are transformed into elements of space; they are inscribed in different temporal phases in space. . . . Space is part of the template itself (the white hollows) and with the black (relief surfaces) it constructs this print of a neoconcrete nature.[19]

The primary aim of Pape's relatively short statement seems to have been to relate her woodcuts to the neoconcrete group's goals by elaborating on the ways her prints dynamically exceed their two-dimensionality and expand into topological space. But by the time she took this issue up again in a 1975 text, she had long left printmaking behind and could reflect on the development of her work in that medium in a manner that placed it in the broader trajectory of her artistic practice.

> The woodcut presented itself to me initially as a black surface. On it I opened rays of light. The figure began to appear. The figure or some other thing moving in the background. I continued consuming (that is, opening slices of light) until I completed the object in the engraving. . . . I dug away at the black until I got to the white, which was, in fact, external space.[20]

Pape had evidently realized that her larger project when working with constructive woodcuts had been to unveil the internal elements of that medium—through cuts, bores, scrapes, and slices into printing blocks of different grains of wood— and arrive at its apotheosis: the generation of light and its dissemination through space. But by now she had flipped the notion of opening up a topological virtual space dependent upon an optical form of vision and illusory depth. Instead, she maintained that what the prints had achieved was a haptic visuality, one that draws spectators in close and leads them to lose their sense of proportion to the point where the distinction between virtual and actual space collapses.[21] In the process, not only light but space too came to function as media. Hence the woodcut explorations came to be seen as research into the problems of space, and in this sense, the process that they explored was finite, with a beginning and an end. "My work refers specifically to spatial investigation," she explained in a 1979 statement that linked her engravings to her subsequent production, continuing:

> . . . space being warped, yarn weaving space; the principle of ambiguity, no privileged position for a base or bottom (a work could be inverted without being stripped of all its characteristics), surface pared down to black as color, and the wood's pores acting as vibration to the point of reaching total white: both black and white were always *form* and never figure and ground, since both had a position of *two-dimensionality* and *topological*

aspects. The moment I arrived at total white, I reached the end of my investigations.[22]

Her investigations ended at the moment of unmediated visual reality, the instant when the black space that was overlaid on top of the white was completely "peeling off" and the underlying light was revealed to the eyes.[23]

Line and light were the decisive elements of the process of engraving that Pape used to bring the spectator close enough to the print that figure and ground commingle, and expose the real or literal space that connects the woodcut to the world. This was a means of "investigating reality, a form of knowledge," as she put it in a discussion in which she disavows the aesthetics of printmaking as such: "[M]y research [in the medium of woodcut engraving] focused on the problem of space. Dynamic space. . . . [M]y prints exist primarily as research rather than aesthetic contemplation."[24] Pape came to understand the spatial dimensions that her art opens up as qualities that encompass not only formal activity—"unfolded, twisted, inverted"—but, even more importantly, interactions within the social and institutional context.[25]

BOOKWORKS

The correspondence between the concrete, physical tactility of art and its opposite—namely figurative space—would preoccupy Pape for many years. As she moved from the medium of woodcut prints to dance, bookworks, graphic design, filmmaking, performance, collage, sculptural models, and installations, her production was consistently organized around the exploration of spatial relationships, and in particular the materiality of haptic representation. As a key member of the neoconcrete movement in the late 1950s and early 1960s, she began to produce artworks that appeared to the spectator as projects with which she or he interacts, rather than illusions into which to enter. This type of art called upon a sort of embodied intelligence that could negotiate surrounding space: performative experiments where the sensorial became the fundamental agent of the creative process, and viewer participation the central premise in the reception of art. From this perspective, the spectator comes to know the world more through the senses and corporeal experience than through vision and the mental operations of symbolization. This is a form of spectatorship that is so engaged with the present

that it cannot recede into cognition; a form of experience that can only be described indirectly, and that posits a thin membrane, a skin, that must be pressed up against, between the subject and the world, or the spectator and the artwork. Pape termed this phenomenon "epidermization" (*epidermização*), a neologism that she mobilized to elucidate her working method as well as the tactile visuality upon which her art was dependent. As she put it in a 1976 text: "It is not a discourse or a thesis. I unfold the project at the level of an epidermization of an idea, the sensorial as a form of knowledge and consciousness."[26] This was, therefore, an embodied spectatorship that acknowledged the role of the corporal in the act of seeing and knowing, a spectatorship in which the senses and the intellect are not separate.

The epidermization of ideas, which as I've suggested can already be detected on the surface Pape's prints, is also manifest in the artist's two neoconcrete ballets (1959–60), and her series of bookworks (*Livro da criação*, Book of Creation, 1959–60; *Livro do tempo*, Book of Time, 1960–65; and *Livro da arquitetura*, Book of Architecture, 1959–60). A case in point is the *Livro da criação*, comprised of thirty-square-centimeter units of colored shapes, all of them extending beyond the plane into space. The project presents a formal account of the creation of the world. The narrative is highly conceptual, and the book features very few words. It summons a tactile epistemology as it calls upon the spectator to handle and assemble the various "pages" according to his or her own experience. By appealing to the spectator as an object with which she or he interacts rather than an illusion into which to enter, the *Livro da criação* calls upon an embodied intelligence. It involves thinking with the epidermis, the skin, or giving as much significance to the physical presence of the artwork as to its meaning. The spectator is required to grasp the colorful object, to bring it close, in a look that is so intensely involved with the tangible presence of the book that it cannot take the step back to distinguish figure and ground. It is a visuality that is perpetually contingent, lacking an immobile, outside point of reference. It creates an embodied economy of looking that constructs an intersubjective relationship between the spectator and the artwork, with the former relinquishing her or his own separateness from the latter. "I invented *Livro da criação* in which I recounted the creation of the world non-verbally, with shapes and colors alone," the artist explained. "As you handle the book you are putting together structures and your 'reading' takes place through its colored shapes."[27]

Pape's increasing emphasis on embodied spectatorship would lead her further in the direction of participatory projects, to large-scale works such as *Divisor* (Divider) and *Roda dos prazeres* (Wheel of Pleasures), both 1967. The former consists of a large sheet of white fabric with a grid of several dozen holes cut into it. Each of these equally spaced, buttonhole-like slits is just large enough for the head of a participant to penetrate, thereby bringing together dozens of people to generate the performative artwork. The sheet literalized the notion of epidermization. Pape clarified that *Divisor* was initially meant to take the form of a giant plastic awning, with slits pierced in a large grid, installed above an exhibition space. The plan was to arrange the tarpaulin so that it was lower towards the entryway; as a visitor entered the room he or she would be encouraged to insert their head through one of the holes. In addition, mirrors were to be installed on either side of the huge expanse of fabric, and fans directed to blow cold air overhead and warm air below. The original aim, according to the artist (writing at a later date), was to allude to the alienation of modern life, the obstacles to communication faced by people who, though in close proximity, remain socially isolated from each other and barely interact.[28]

Although this scheme was ultimately left unrealized, Pape staged an altered version of *Divisor* in 1968 in a public space near a Rio de Janeiro favela. There, she brought together neighborhood children and organized them into inserting their heads through the openings of a thirty-square-meter stretch of white fabric. The children, their bodies obscured by the large white plane, were instructed to walk forward, creating what curator Ivana Bentes describes as "a crowd monster with dozens of heads."[29] "There is no work: there is only the unfolding into a thousand routes," Pape wrote about this version of *Divisor*, which she characterized as "the skin of ALL: smooth like a cloud: loose."[30] The children spoke to each other throughout the entire duration of the performance.

The *Roda dos prazeres* (fig. 5) is equally interactive, though the senses it engages additionally include taste.[31] The composition consists of a group of porcelain bowls of differently colored fluids treated with food-coloring and flavoring;

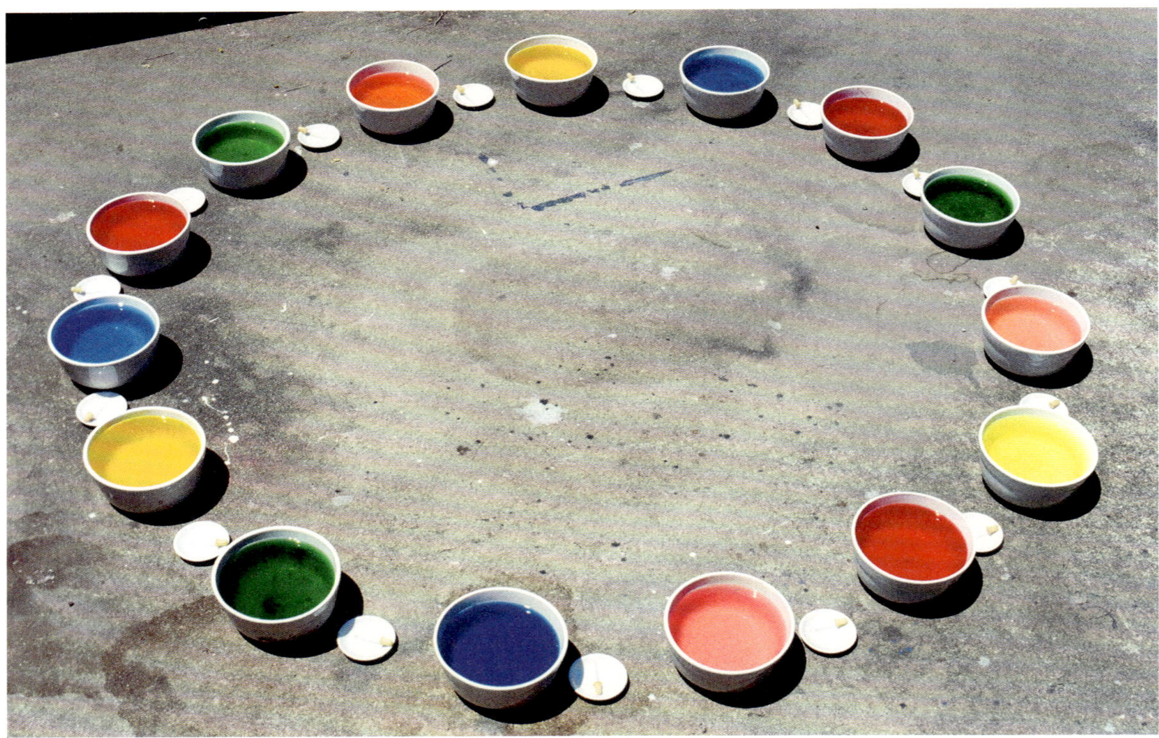

—fig. 5 *Roda dos prazeres* (Wheel of Pleasures), 1967

the vessels are arranged in a circle and each is equipped with its own medicine dropper. Participants are encouraged to partake in this banquet by squeezing the rubber top of the dropper with their fingertips, putting the tip of the dropper into a bowl, releasing the grip on the top so that the pressure inside sucks up some of the liquid, and then dripping drops of the colored solutions—which feature both pleasant and unpleasant tastes—onto their tongues. "In this way," Pape wrote about *Roda dos prazeres* in 1980, "an ambivalence of the senses was created: the eye saw one thing and was delighted, but the tongue might reject it. Or it could reinforce what the eye had already devoured, couldn't it?"[32] Photographs of participants engaging with the piece (see fig. 6) capture alternating senses of pleasure and pain. Needless to say, Pape's claim that "the most radical experience in *Roda dos prazeres* would be the use of poison as one of the flavors" only increases the work's ambivalence.[33]

IRON RELIEF SCULPTURES

The seductive power of color also characterizes Pape's series of *Amazoninos*, which the artist began to make in 1989, the same year

she assumed a professorship at the Escola de Belas Artes of the Universidade Federal do Rio de Janeiro. These large, wall-hung, abstract sculptures combine several of her concerns during this time, including questions of space, volume, function (and its deviation), movement, color, and the plasticity of materials. The title of the series is at once euphonic, attentive to the sound of syllables uttered one after the other ("A/ma/zo/ni/nos"), and mindful of the vast natural landscape of Brazil, which was a central theme of Pape's master's thesis. Apparently, Pape arrived at the title while looking out the window of an airplane flying over the Amazon jungle, though the brilliant red of the *Amazoninos Vermelho* (especially two from 1989, ills. pp. 76, 77 and 92, 93, that feature protruding, rounded shapes), summons the hue of something much more specific: the flower of the achiote, a shrub found in the tropical regions of Brazil. The achiote, which the indigenous Tupinambá people referred to as *urucum*, produces seeds that they have long used to make body paint. Either way, the resulting forms are as organic as they are geometric, and, combined with their pulsating colors, reorganize the visual and spatial fields: they explode the surface on which they hang. Some, such as

Amazonino Vermelho e Preto, 1990 (ills. pp. 67, 68, 69) or *Amazonino Vermelho*, 1989 (ills. pp. 86, 87), engage their surroundings in a physical manner. Like carnivorous plants, the long, bright tentacles of these artworks threaten to ensnare the passing visitor.

The *Amazoninos* disrespect the properties of their metal medium. Iron—inherent with heaviness and solidity—is shaped into forms that seem as gentle and malleable as paper. This surprising result transgresses the constituent limits of the material, and in some cases mobilizes metal to figure a locus of emanating light lines not unlike those that her earlier *Tecelares* put into play. In *Amazonino Vermelho*, 1989 (fig. 7, ills. pp. 70, 71), for example, a flood of thin, line-like tentacles breaks forward from the square iron plate that functions as the picture plane. This opens up not only a more dynamic relationship with the spectator but also a greater interaction between the art object and the architectural space in which it is displayed. A similar effect is created by *Amazonino Vermelho* (fig. 8, ills. pp. 88, 89) and *Amazonino Vermelho* (ills. pp. 72, 73), both 1989, which collapse the qualities of hardness and softness, inertness and motion, rigidity and droopiness, into equivalent categories.

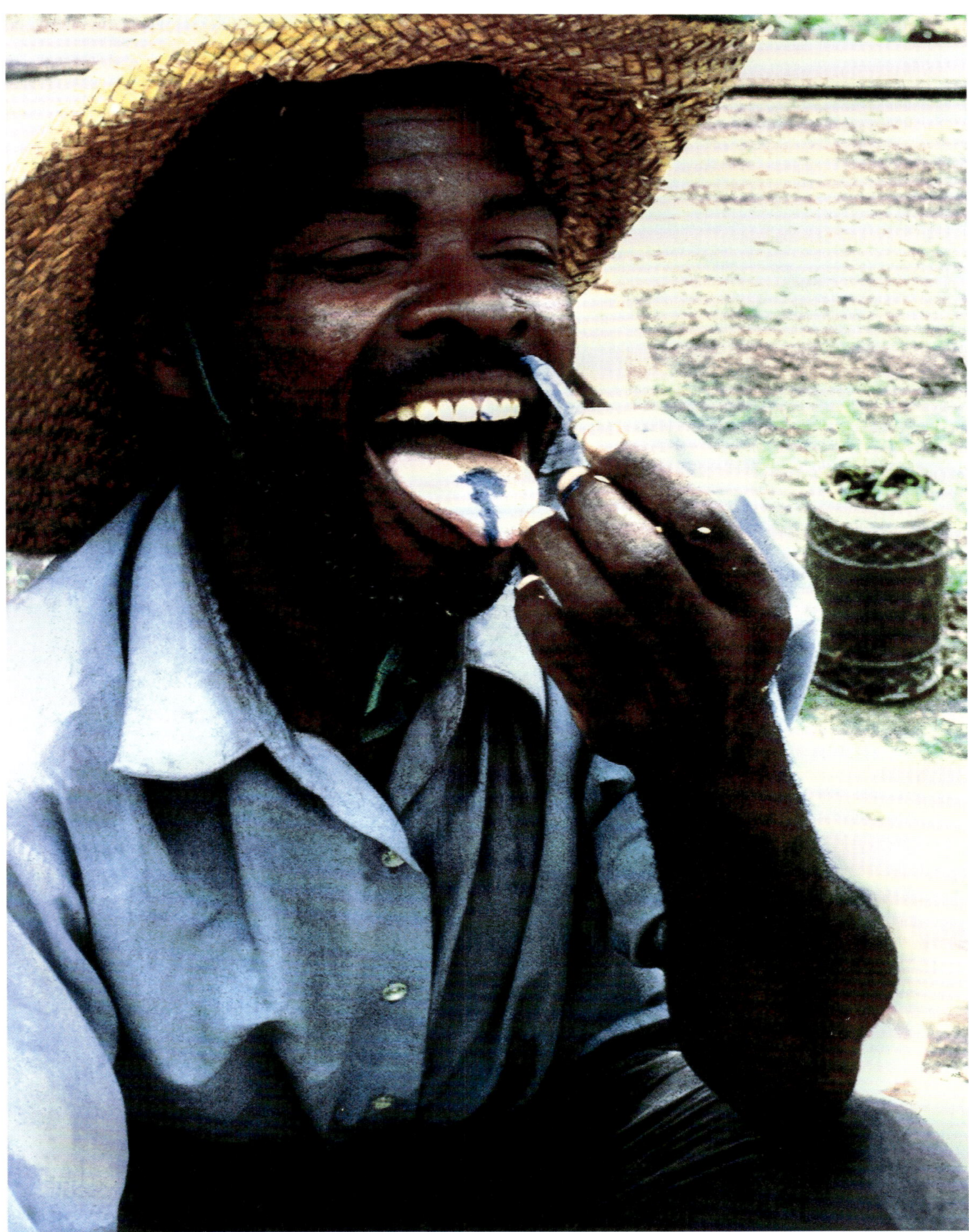

—fig. 6 *Mineiro* (Miner), 1968

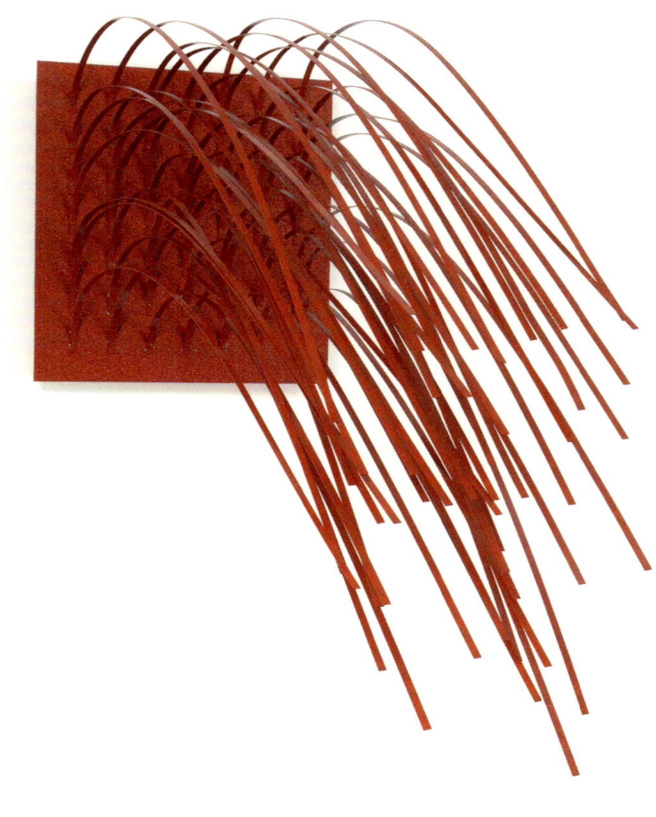

—fig. 7 *Amazonino Vermelho* (Red Amazonino), 1989/2003

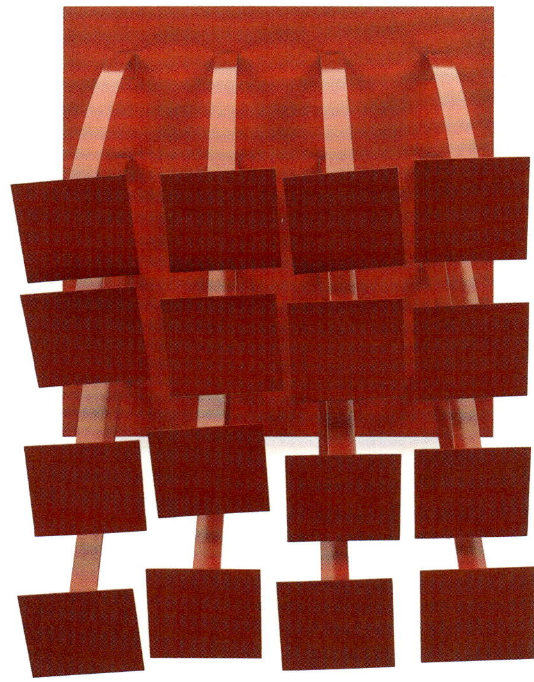

—fig. 8 *Amazonino Vermelho* (Red Amazonino), 1989/2003

Pape occasionally worked with three-dimensional paper models when designing the *Amazoninos*. In this sense, these iron sculptures echo books such as the *Livro da criação*, which protrudes from the wall in a relief-like manner. Yet, while the game, or element of play, that the bookworks set in motion invites the spectator to participate and invent, to carry out his or her own permutations and combinations, the *Amazoninos* invert this operation. It is almost as if the artwork now mobilizes the spectator. The shadows cast by dangling tentacles and other protuberances, and the intensity of the vibrant color that characterizes the *Amazoninos*, blur distinctions: between the cold inertness of the iron material and the powerful organicity connoted by the combination of colors and forms; and in the sensory and temporal experience of the passing viewer, problematizing and turning these elements inside out, and thereby giving these artworks a life of their own.

WEBBING AND WEAVING

"A strange link exists" between the different media that Pape uses, wrote Oiticica in 1969. Common threads run through her work, like a "spider's web."[34] Indeed, "webbing" and its close companion "weaving," became operative metaphors for the artist when she spoke about her work from this time, and through the 1980s. *Ttéia*, a project that initially began as a series of nets between trees for children's play, was further developed by Pape in experiments carried out with her students at the Universidade Santa Úrsula in Rio de Janeiro's Parque Lage during the 1970s.[35] The project eventually evolved into complex installations of threads and lights in space. Teaching at Santa Úrsula, Pape became increasingly interested in a type of experimental pedagogy that involved taking her students to different parts of Rio de Janeiro. She recollected that these journeys through the city with her students, most often by automobile, led her to discover

> a new type of relationship with urban space, as if I were a spider of sorts, weaving space. After all, I start from a certain point, then go across, and turn, go up and down overpasses, go in and out of tunnels. . . . It was as if we now enjoyed an aerial view of the city that was like an enormous cobweb, a huge entanglement.[36]

She took to referring to such entanglements as "magnetized spaces" (*espacos imantados*), because "the whole thing seemed alive, and I moved inside it, pulling up a thread to be woven and wound into an endless skein."[37]

Pape outlined the *Ttéia* in an important 1979 text, "Ttéia. Área abierta" (Open Area), further elaborating on this concept of "magnetized space": experiencing the meshing procedure involves "rising in the air, having only a frayed lightweight fabric as support, with light shining through it, like strands of color of its own structure-threads." Movement "upward or downward, to and fro, not restricted to a single point of view" invokes an "apprehension of space and objects" that is tactile and haptic, and requires an active spectator.[38] She explains that the project is "part of a collective movement in which the structural installation is completed through viewer involvement. To this end, the project will have a coordinator (Lygia Pape), a craft weaver, and assistants." The goal was to mesh together a zone in which extraordinary things could occur:

> The proposal is to "weave a space" as part of a creative process that will establish new relationships between creative artists and those viewers who will be appropriating it. . . . [T]he

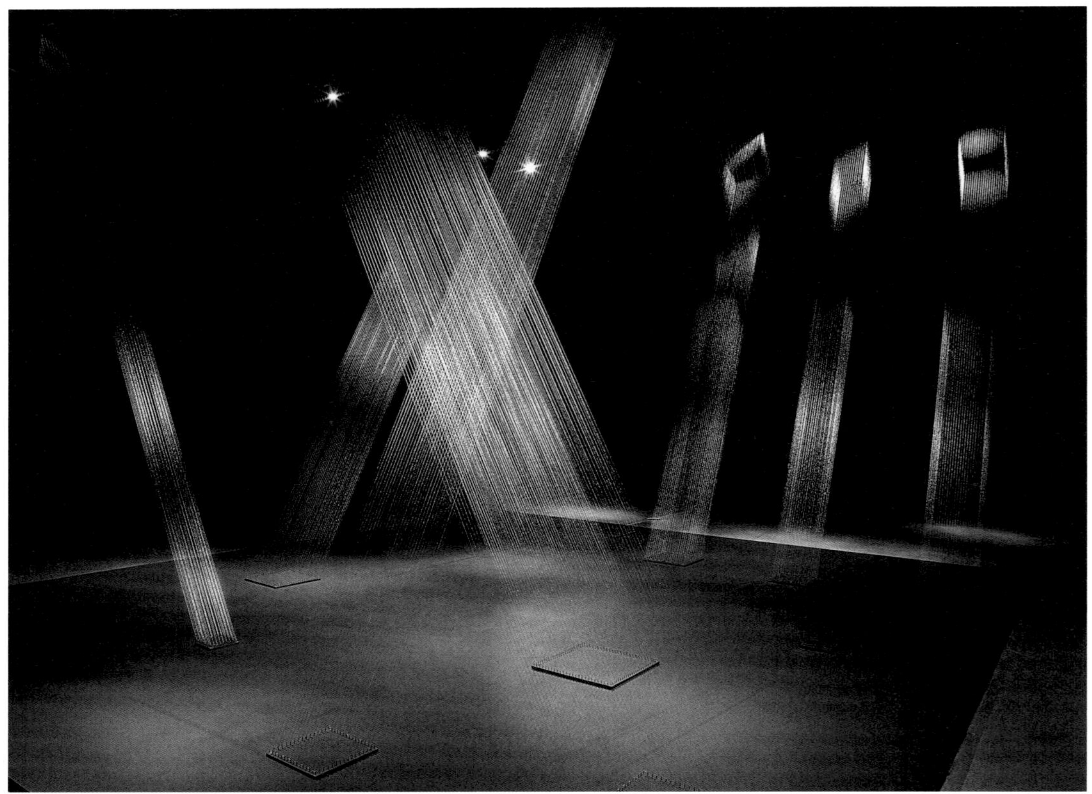

—fig. 9 *Ttéia 1, C*, 2001/2016

idea is to broaden new perceptions, new horizons from which lines generated by the web structure will emerge and grow in the actual place in which it is in use. Before there was nothing, and after there is just the idea and perceptions conveyed through SPIDER WEBBING.[39]

Accordingly, by "magnetized space" Pape refers to the energy "generated" by the complex interaction of forms, shapes, and spectators in the production of an artwork. Magnetic space pulls the spectator into its force field, privileging material presence and a palpable visuality that appeals to the body as a whole.

This theory of magnetic space led Pape to relate the *Ttéia* works to "experiences of walking in labyrinths (through forest vegetation or between buildings), occupying space with stretched colored yarn in such a way that gradually [the lines of yarn] will intersect and form primary structures."[40] As with a labyrinth—which by definition consists of an expanse that is contingent, intimate, perpetually immediate, and lacking an immobile outside point of reference—Pape's magnetized spaces, the cobwebs and convoluted entanglements, formulate the environment in an undifferentiated way. Within these spaces,

the visual boundaries between body and world may feel indistinct: the tangled threads of the web may encompass one's limbs or shadow. Magnetized space requires the spectator to work intuitively and haptically to constitute the form, to bring it forth from latency. As in earlier works such as *Livro da criação*, it constructs an intersubjective relationship between the spectator and the forms in space. The spectator is called upon to fill the gaps of the entanglement, to engage with the multiple threads of the cobweb. By interacting up-close with the elements in that space, close enough that figure and ground commingle— just as in the haptic visuality of her woodcut *Tecelares*—the beholder relinquishes her or his own sense of separateness from those forms.

Pape also used the title *Ttéia* for a series of artworks she started in 1977. These sculptures consist of many parallel gold- or silver-plated copper filaments, interlaced symmetrically top to bottom on square metal frames, in a way that echoes and extends the parallel white lines of the alluring 1950s engravings and the dynamic lines of the captivating *Amazoninos* of the 1980s—lines that seem to move on the plane and already suggest a projection into space. When expanded to majestic, room-size installation, the gold- or

silver-plated threads capture the light in such a way that they come to resemble massive beams of luminescence emanating from above and striking the ground this way and that, from ceiling to floor (fig. 9). The effect is enhanced to operatic proportion when the exhibition space is darkened and spotlights are directed on the striated clusters of strings. Smaller iterations of the *Ttéia 1* sculptures, such as *Ttéia 1, C: Metallic #1* (ills. pp. 111, 112, 113) or *Ttéia 1, C: Metallic #3* (ills. pp. 116, 117), both 2003, function in a similar way, though relatively pared down: they each feature two forty-nine-centimeter-tall beams, delicately tilted to the point of equilibrium between standing upright and collapsing altogether, their acute tentativeness suggesting that they will succumb to the slightest movement, or breath of air. The angled arrays of illuminated thread of the two beams seem to intersect and pass through one another, and a kind of rhythmic, pulsing optical interference plays on the eyes of the spectator as he or she circumnavigates the objects.

Recalling the woodcuts and bookworks of the artist's earlier production, the extraordinarily seductive *Ttéia 1* sculptures, effecting a peculiar fascination and fragility, are presented as objects with which to interact rather than illusions to enter. The interplay with light on the thread-like filaments, which alternately glow and disappear, shifting as the spectator progresses around the artworks, elicits an oscillation between not only materiality and ephemerality, but also optical and palpable ways of seeing. These bright and reflective webs summon the spectators and compel them to relinquish their own sense of separateness from the world.

A PLURI-SENSORIAL ART

Art historian Adele Nelson has shown that, at around the same time that Pape commenced the *Ttéia 1*, the artist began to refer to the 1950s engravings in wood as "Tecelares," which in English roughly translates into "weavings," thereby consolidating the trajectory of her work by establishing a direct relationship between the early prints and the then-new sculptures that she would continue to produce until the end of her life.[41] Much of Pape's artistic production—both of these bodies of work, the ballets and books of the late 1950s and early 1960s, participatory experiments of later that decade, and her iron relief sculptures of the late 1980s and 1990s—can be seen as an attempt to break the figure/ground binary by imagining the reversed possibility of a pictorial plane; she conceives of space as capable of virtually (in the prints), and then physically (in the sculptures), activating the viewer's participatory and embodied experience. Her pluri-sensorial works appeal especially to a more tactile, bodily form of perception. Space, from this perspective, functions metaphorically as the epidermis of the world, "like the skin of a whale," against which the spectator presses up when negotiating the precarious relationship between interiority and exteriority, perception and conception; it is the threshold between intuition and consciousness, sense experience and knowledge.

1. See interview with Lygia Pape in Fernando Cocchiarale and Anna Bella Geiger, eds., *Abstracionismo, geometrico e informal: A vanguard brasileira nos anos cinqüenta* (Rio de Janeiro: Funarte, Instituto Nacional de Artes Plásticas, 1987), 153–54. The Brazilian art scene that Pape encountered in the early 1950s was also strongly mediated by the presence of critic Mário Pedrosa in Rio de Janeiro. Pedrosa, who had an expertise in gestalt theory, had recently joined artists Almir Mavignier, Ivan Serpa, and Abraham Palatnik in running an arts therapy workshop commenced by Dr. Nise da Silveira at the psychiatric center in Engenho de Dentro, a neighborhood on the outskirts of Rio de Janeiro. Dissatisfied by the violent methods of psychiatric treatment still in use during the 1940s, Dr. Nise da Silveira found in occupational therapy, including arts therapy, another way to treat schizophrenia. She initially turned to Mavignier to supervise the arts studio, which opened in the fall of 1946. Mavignier soon included Pedrosa and the other artists in the studio classes offered. For more on the arts therapy workshop, which included exhibitions and site visits, see Luiz Carlos Mello, "Nise da Silveira and the Artists of Engenho de Dentro," trans. Clifford Landers, *Review: Literature and Arts of the Americas* 39, no. 2 (2006): 270–76.

2. As Pape would later recall, "My professional relationship with the plastic arts actually began when the Museu de Arte Moderna, Rio de Janeiro (MAM-RJ), was inaugurated. Ivan Serpa was already teaching classes there, but I didn't study under him. I met Serpa through Décio Vieira, and, little by little, we began to meet people and create a circle of friends with common interests." Lygia Pape, in "Birds of Marvelous Colors: Lygia Pape Interviewed by Lúcia Carneiro and Ileana Pradilla," 1997, in Iria Candela et al., eds., *Lygia Pape: A Multitude of Forms*, exh. cat. (New York: Metropolitan Museum of Art, 2017), 16.

3. The Museu de Art Moderna, Rio de Janeiro, was at the time housed in the Ministry of Education and Health building.

4. As Briony Fer has explained: "Both *Tecleares* and *Ttéia* are words that [Pape] coined and are notoriously hard to translate. . . . *Tecelar* stems from *tecer*, to weave. . . *teia* can mean something precious or delicate, but also a web." Briony Fer, "Slits, eyes, geometries," in *Lygia Pape,* exh. cat. (New York: Hauser & Wirth London, 2017), 20.

5. Pape takes these issues up in "Gravura: Depoimento de Lygia Pape," 1959, translated as "On Printmaking: A Statement by Lygia Pape" in *Lygia Pape: Magnetized Space*, exh. cat. (Madrid, Spain: Museo Nacional Centro de Arte Reina Sofía, 2011), 85.

6. Describing the technique in a 1975 text, Pape emphasizes the many senses mobilized: "The sensory sound of a roller spreading out paint was part of the creative process. The haptic experience with the material, the instruments—gravers, rice paper template, printing, copying." Lygia Pape, "Quarenta gravuras neoconcretas," 1975, translated as "Forty Neo-Concrete Woodcuts," in *Lygia Pape: Magnetized Space*, 88.

7. Pape, "Gravura: Depoimento de Lygia Pape," in *Lygia Pape: Magnetized Space*, 86.

8. Paulo Herkenhoff, "Lygia Pape: The Art of Passage," in *Lygia Pape: Magnetized Space*, 32.

9. For an overview of Grupo Frente, see Frederico Morais, "GRUPO FRENTE—a primeira turnma," in *Grupo Frente/1954–1956, I Exposição Nacional de Arte Abstrata/1953*, exh. cat. (Rio de Janeiro: Galeria de Arte do BANERJ, 1984), n.p.

10. Yet, according to Herkenhoff, Pape liked to emphasize that she only had a few lessons with Ostrower and that these focused on linocuts. Herkenhoff observes that although Ostrower's prints tended toward the expressionist end of the spectrum, which Pape's never would, some of Ostrower's values were transmitted to Pape, including "art as an ethical act; the technical rigor and the principle of the just measure, or the need to pursue a balance between art's intellectual project and its rendition into works." See Herkenhoff, "The Art of Passage," in *Lygia Pape: Magnetized Space*, 28. Of course, these notions could have also been gleaned from artists such as Serpa, or the critic Pedrosa who by then had been contemplating the notion of art as experience for years. But the fact that Ostrower was espousing these values through engraving must have had an impact on Pape because she became increasingly absorbed in this medium.

11. Pape, "Gravura: Depoimento de Lygia Pape," in *Lygia Pape: Magnetized Space*, 85.

12. Sergio B. Martins, "An Anticlass in Avant-Gardism," in Candela, *Lygia Pape: A Multitude of Forms*, 27.

13. Ibid., 182, fn.10.

14. Fer, "Slits, eyes, geometries," in *Lygia Pape*, 17.

15. Pape, "Quarenta gravuras neoconcretas," in *Lygia Pape: Magnetized Space*, 89.

16. Pape describes the origin of the line in her woodcut prints as follows: "When I saw [through] a wooden board and create a line at the joint of the two resulting sections, I bring into being a relationship that did not exist before. The line thus created is quite different from the line drawn on the sensitive wood fiber or a sanded-down black surface: it relates perfectly to the selected material and the novelty is in the improvement in the quality of the line as demanded by the problem that the artist has agreed to express." Lygia Pape, as cited by Herkenhoff: "The Art of Passage," in *Lygia Pape: Magnetized Space*, 34.

17. Hélio Oiticica, "Tropicália Times Series 2. Lygia Pape," 1969, reproduced in translation in *Lygia Pape: Magnetized Space*, 245.

18. Pape, "Gravura: Depoimento de Lygia Pape," in *Lygia Pape: Magnetized Space*, 85–87.

19. Ibid., 87.

20. Lygia Pape, in Frederico Morais, "A gravura como forma de conhecimento," *O Globo* (Rio de Janeiro), July 21, 1975, as cited in Luiz Camillo Osorio, "Lygia Pape: Experimentation and Resistance," in *Lygia Pape: Magnetized Space*, 99.

21. Here's Pape again: "The woodcut is increasingly gouged, virtual space is annulled, and the print is ever more part of the real space." Pape, "Quarenta gravuras neoconcretas," in *Lygia Pape: Magnetized Space*, 89.

22. Lygia Pape, "Depoimento," 1979, translated as "Statement," in *Lygia Pape: Magnetized Space*, 91. Italics in the original.

23. Ibid.

24. Lygia Pape, in Frederico Morais, "A gravura como forma de conhecimento," 1975, translated as "Printmaking as a Form of Knowledge," in *Lygia Pape: Magnetized Space*, 93.

25. Lygia Pape, "Depoimento. Eat Me: a gula ou a luxúria?", 1976, translated as "Statement. Eat Me: Gluttony or Lust?", in *Lygia Pape: Magnetized Space*, 372.

26. Claudia Calirman, "'Epidermic' and Visceral Works: Lygia Pape and Anna Maria Maiolino," *Women's Art Journal* 35, no. 2 (Fall/Winter 2014): 23.

27. Lygia Pape, in *Lygia Pape* (Rio de Janeiro: Funarte, 1983), as cited in Paulo Venancio Filho, "The Re-Creation of the Book," in *Lygia Pape: Magnetized Space*, 220.

28. Lygia Pape, letter to Guy Brett, September 1988, cited in Guy Brett, "A Permanently Open Seed," in *Lygia Pape: Magnetized Space*, 260.

29. Ivana Bentes, "Chaos-Construction: The Formal and the Sensory in Lygia Pape's Films," in *Lygia Pape: Magnetized Space*, 346.

30. Lygia Pape, "Divisor. A pele de TODOS: lisa, leve como nuvem: solta," 1985, translated as "Divisor. The Skin of All: Smooth, Light Like a Cloud: Loose," in *Lygia Pape: Magnetized Space*, 244.

31. Luiz Camillo Osorio observes that the title is taken from a poem by Brazilian poet Joaquim de Sousa Andrade, better known by his pseudonym Sousândrade. See Osorio, "Experimentation and Resistance," in *Lygia Pape: Magnetized Space*, 111.

32. Lygia Pape, "Catiti Catiti na Terra dos Brasis" [Catiti Catiti in the land of the Brasis/Brazil], Masters dissertation presented to the Philosophy Department at the Universidad Federal do Rio de Janeiro (UFRJ), 1980, as cited in Osorio, "Experimentation and Resistance," in *Lygia Pape: Magnetized Space*, 111.

33. Lygia Pape, in "Birds of Marvelous Colors: Lygia Pape Interviewed by Lúcia Carneiro and Ileana Pradilla," in Candela, *Lygia Pape: A Multitude of Forms*, 22.

34. Oiticica, "Tropicália. Lygia Pape," in *Lygia Pape: Magnetized Space*, 245.

35. See note 4.

36. Lygia Pape, "Espaços imantados," n.d., translated as "Magnetized Spaces," in *Lygia Pape: Magnetized Space*, 285. For a discussion of Pape's pedagogical practice see Lauro Cavalcanti, "Lygia Pape: In Pursuit of the Poem," in *Lygia Pape: Magnetized Space*, 292–303.

37. Ibid., 285.

38. Lygia Pape, "Ttéia. Área abierta," 1979, translated as "Ttéia. Open Area," in *Lygia Pape: Magnetized Space*, 370.

39. Ibid., 370, 369.

40. Ibid., 370.

41. Adele Nelson, "Sensitive and Nondiscursive Things: Lygia Pape and the Reconception of Printmaking," *Art Journal* 71, no. 3 (Fall 2012): 42.

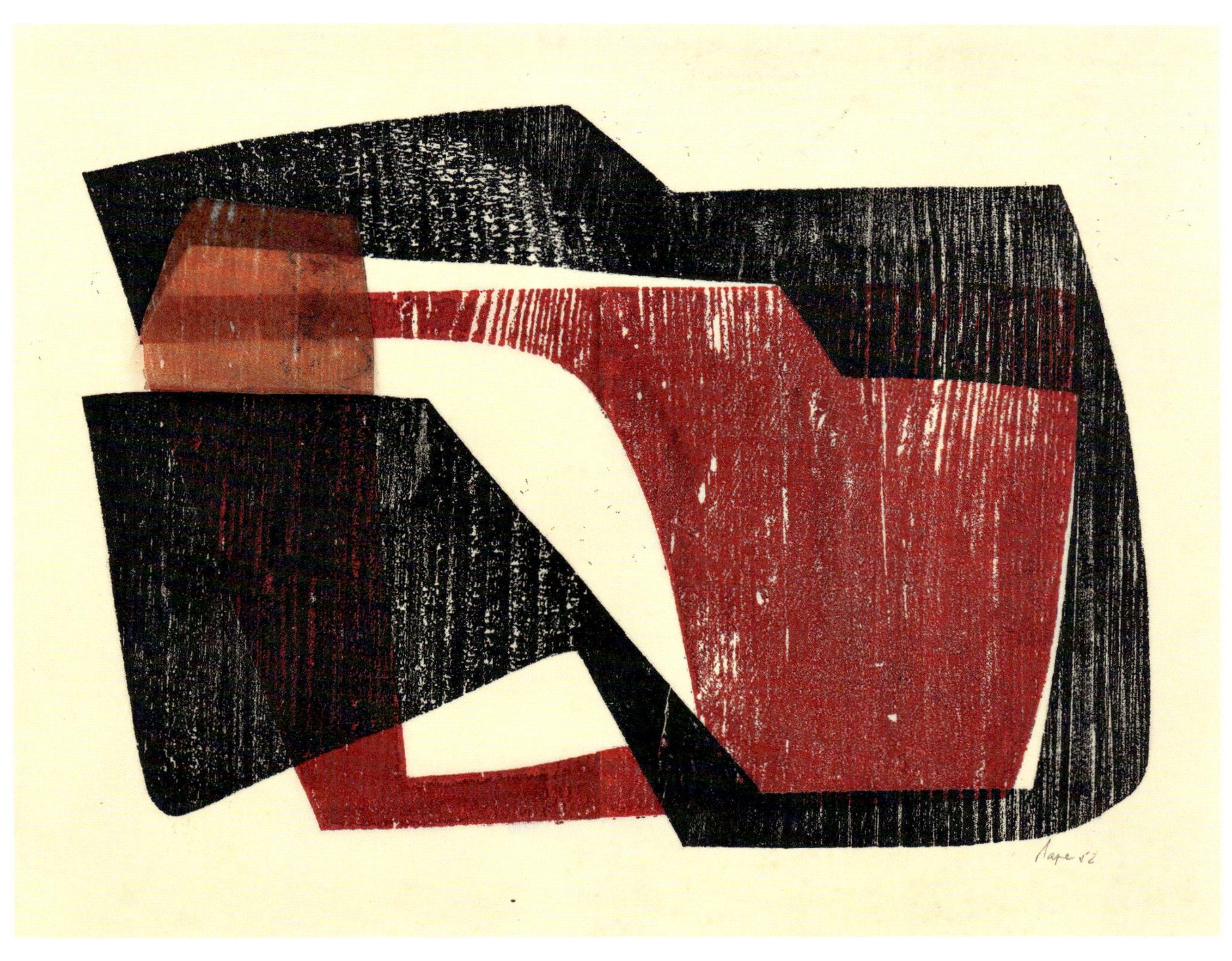

Tecelar, 1952

Tecelar, 1954

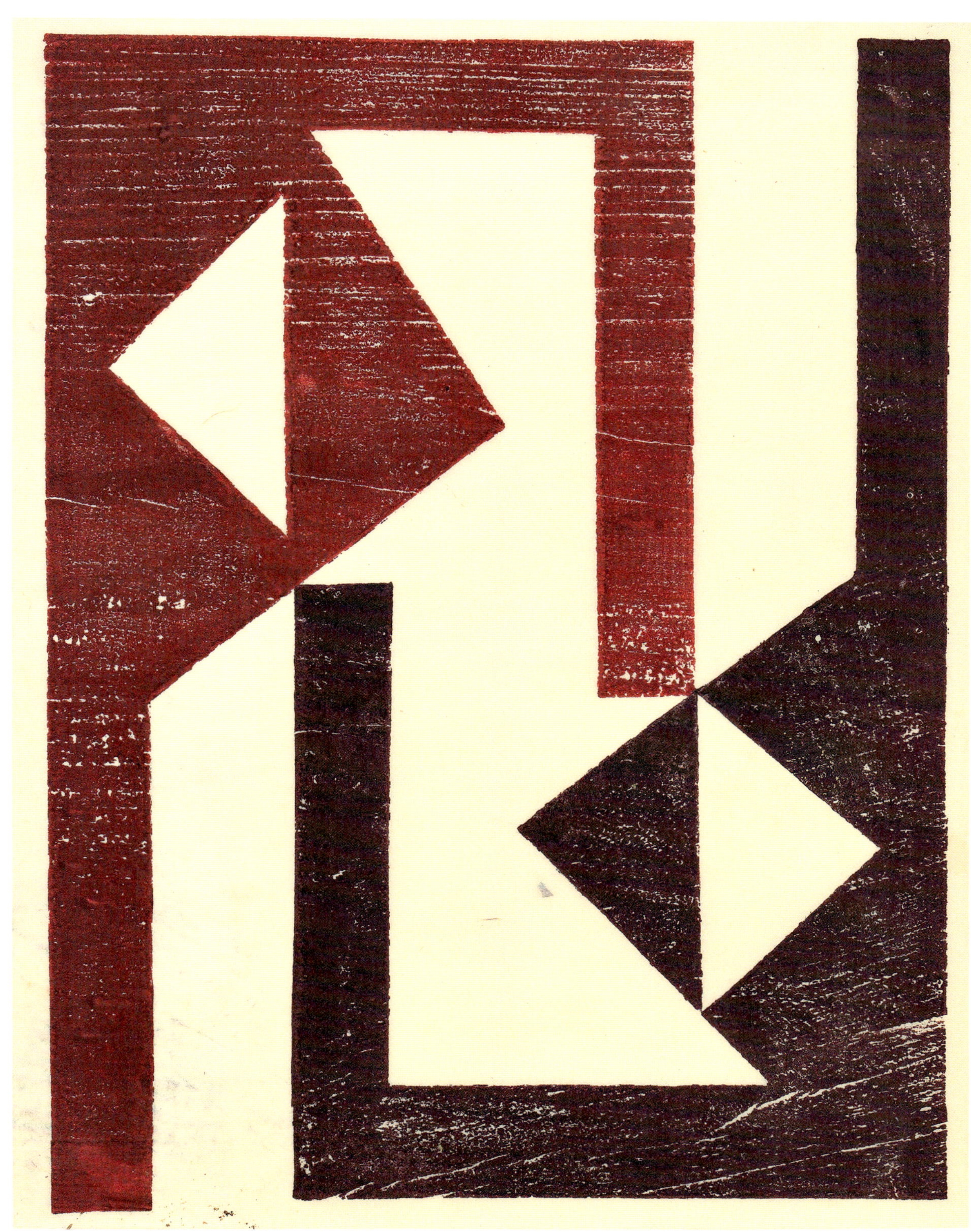

Tecelar, 1955

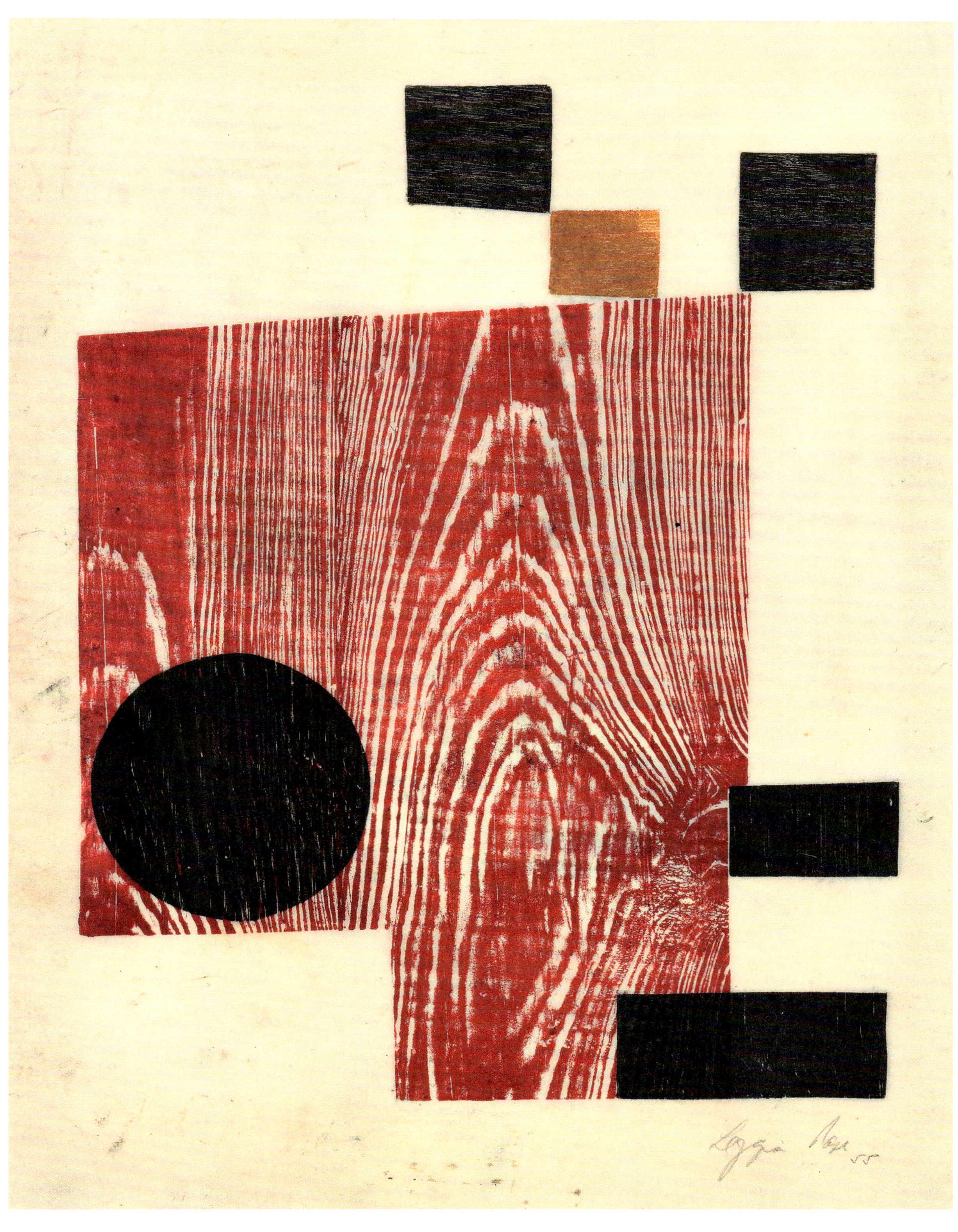

Tecelar, 1953

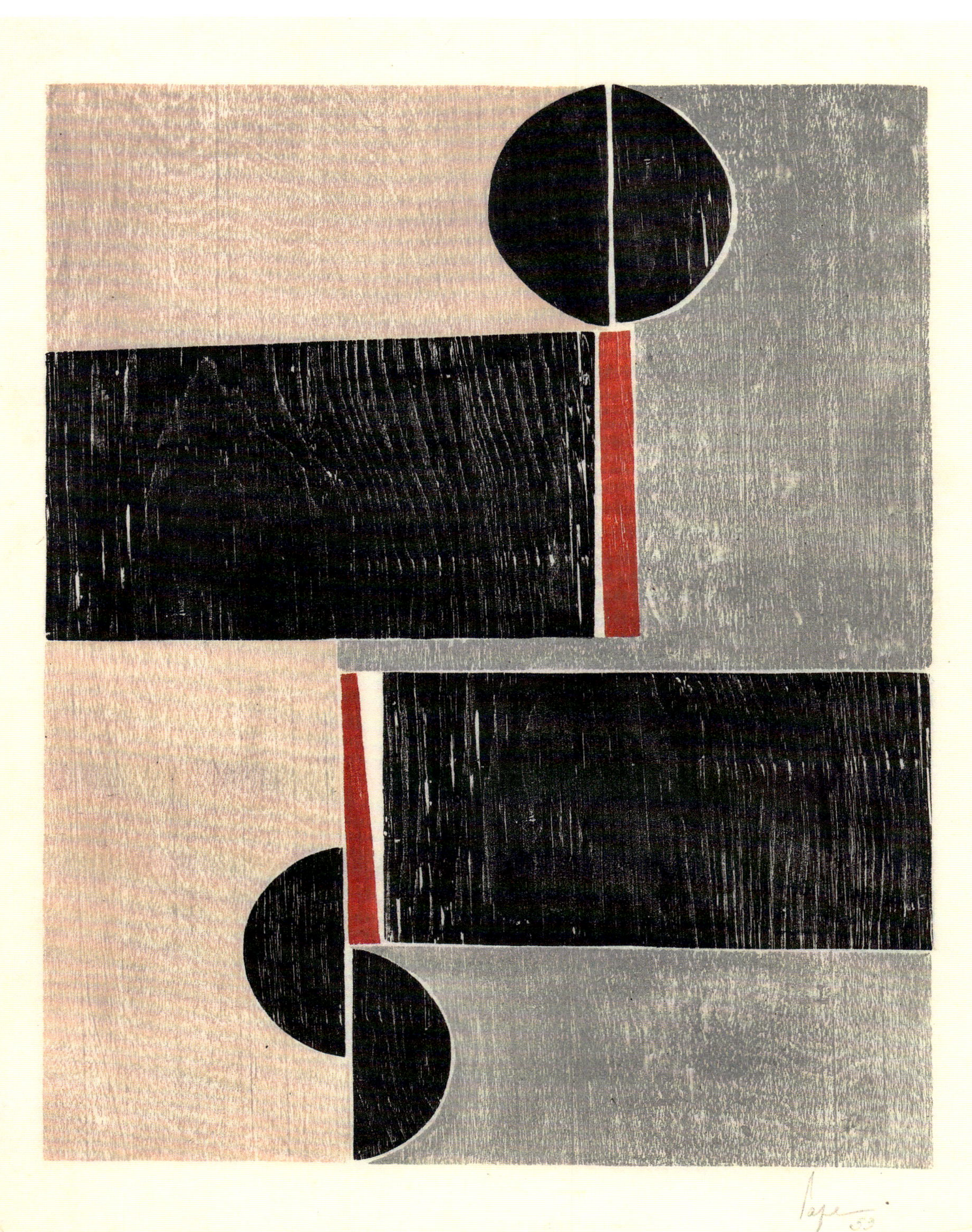

Tecelar, 1953

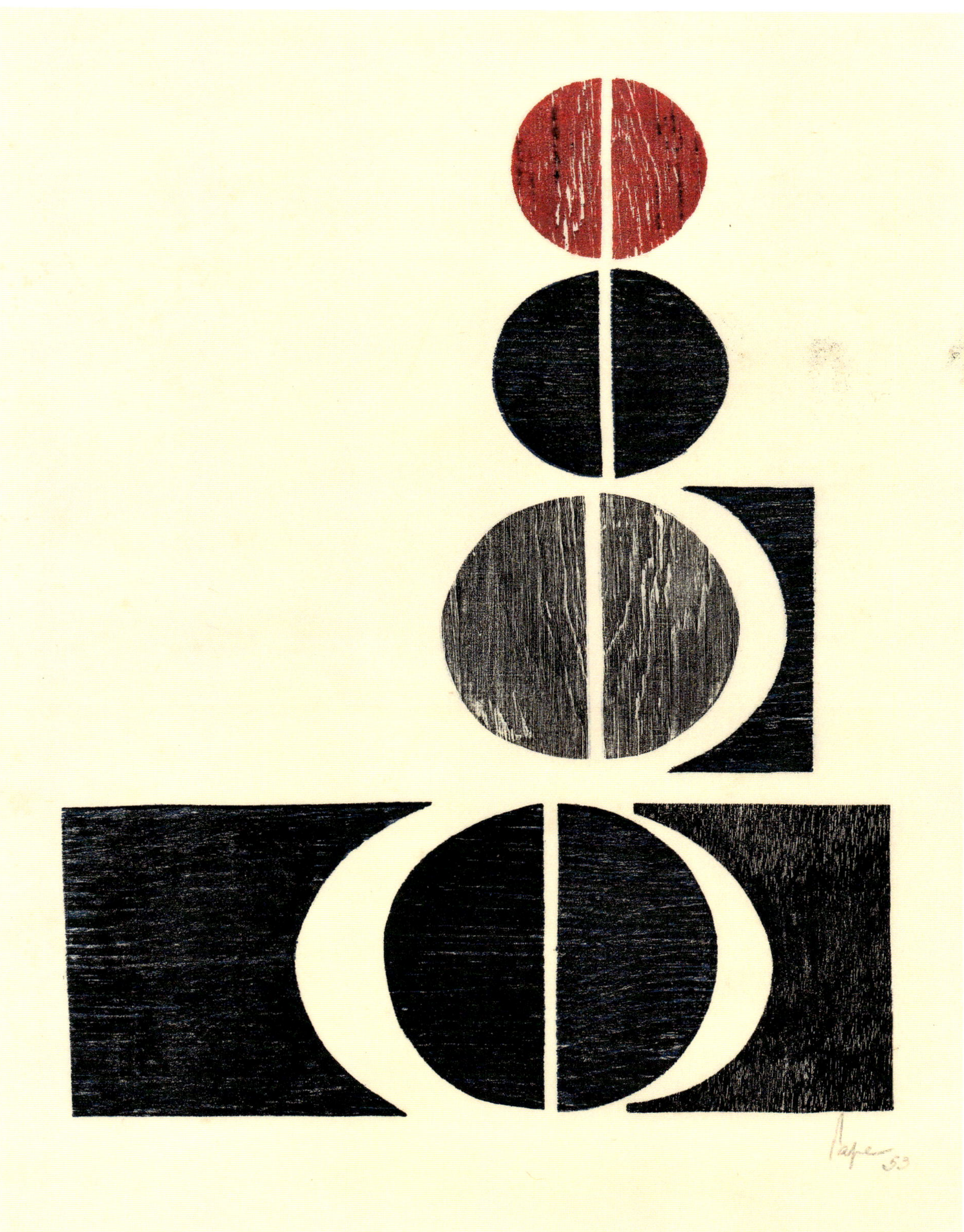

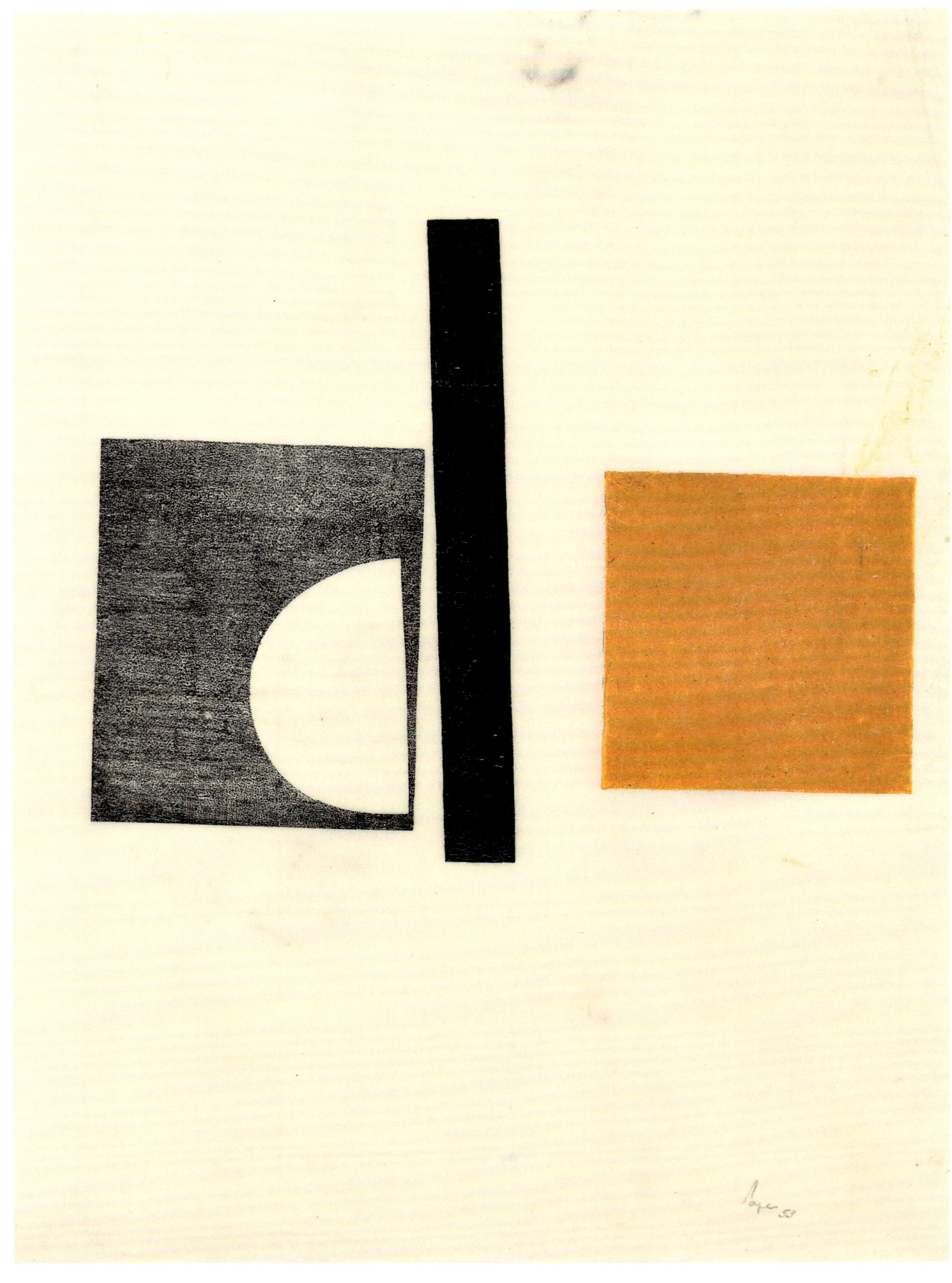

Tecelar, 1953

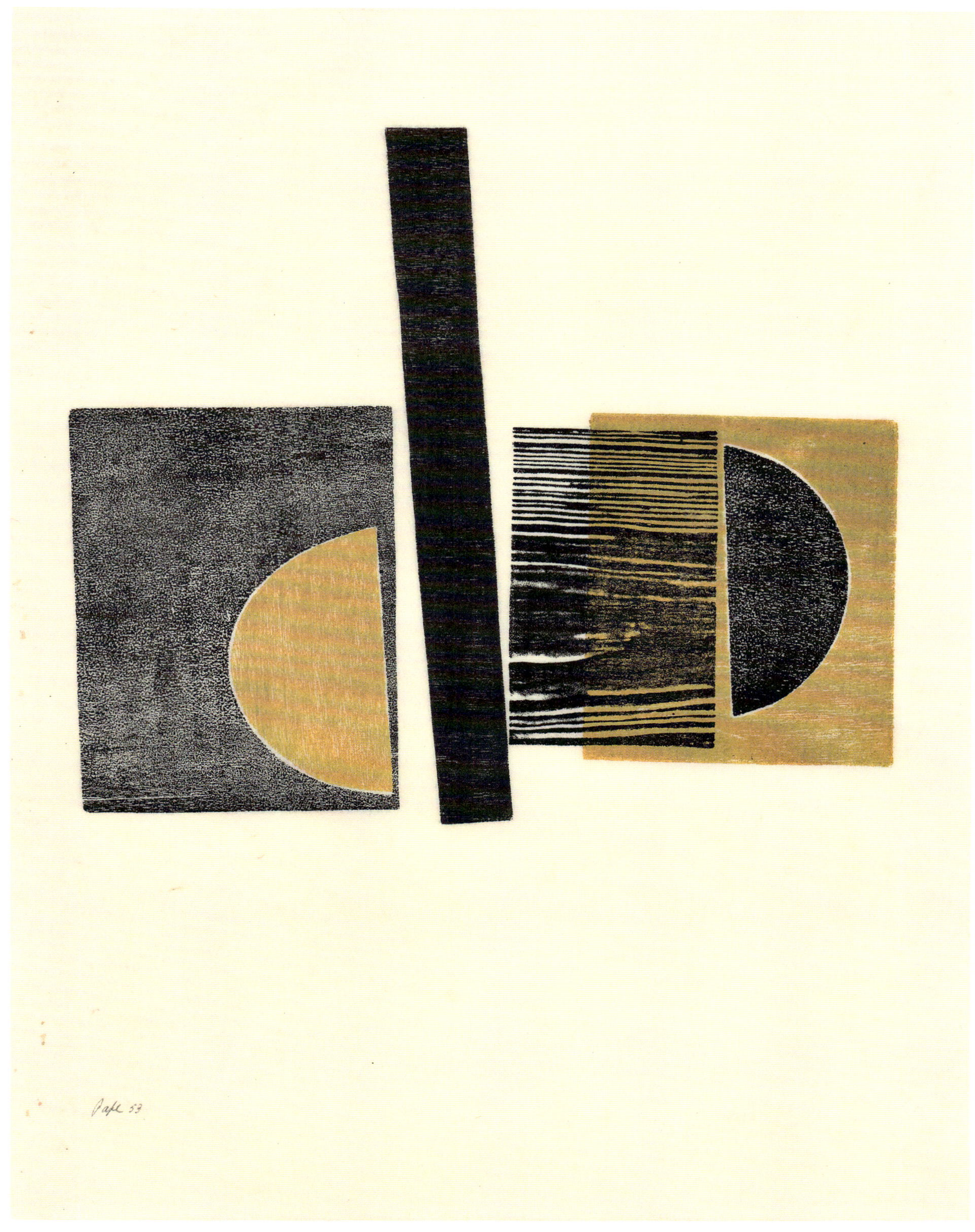

Tecelar, 1953

Tecelar, 1957

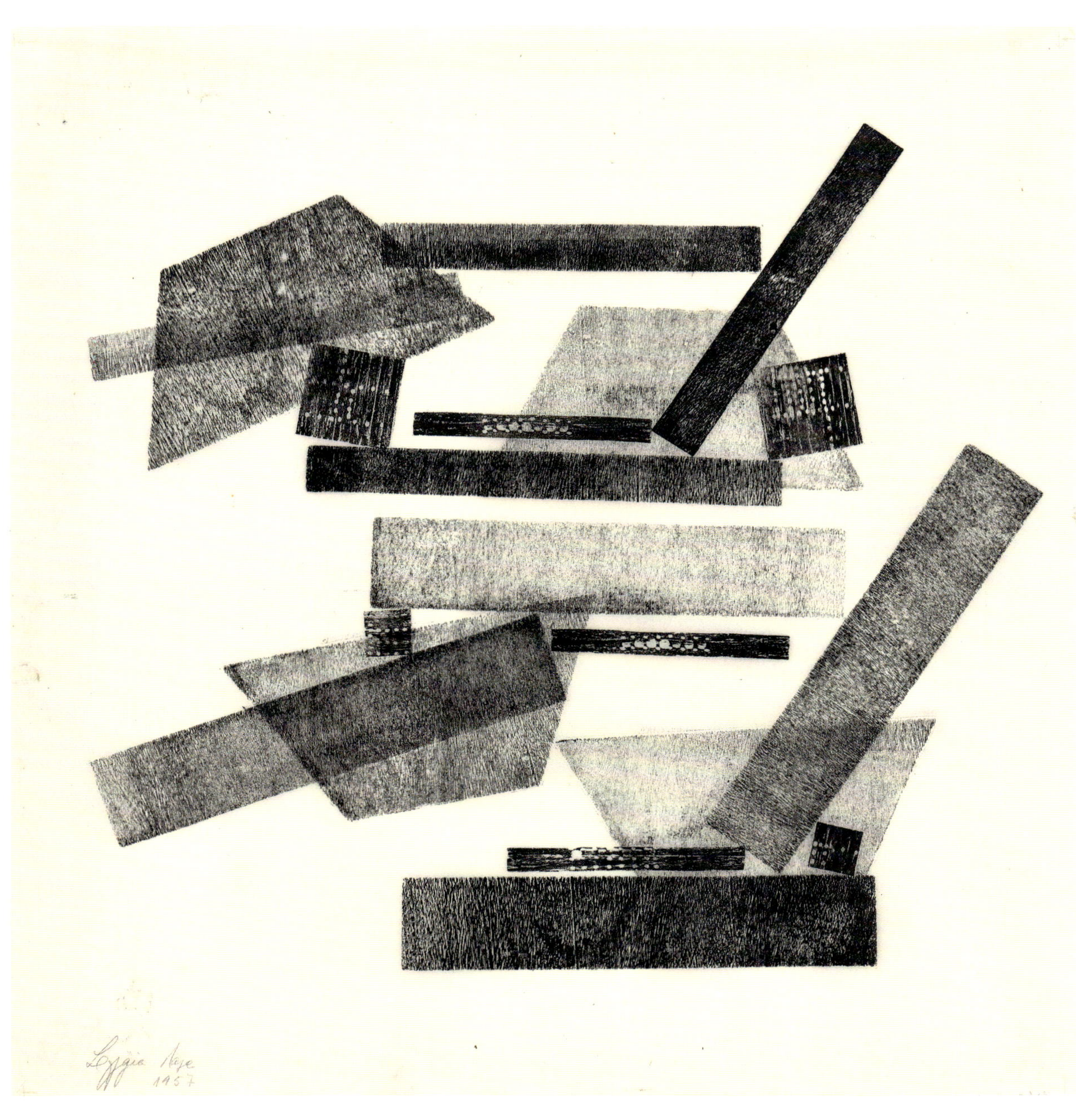

Tecelar, 1955

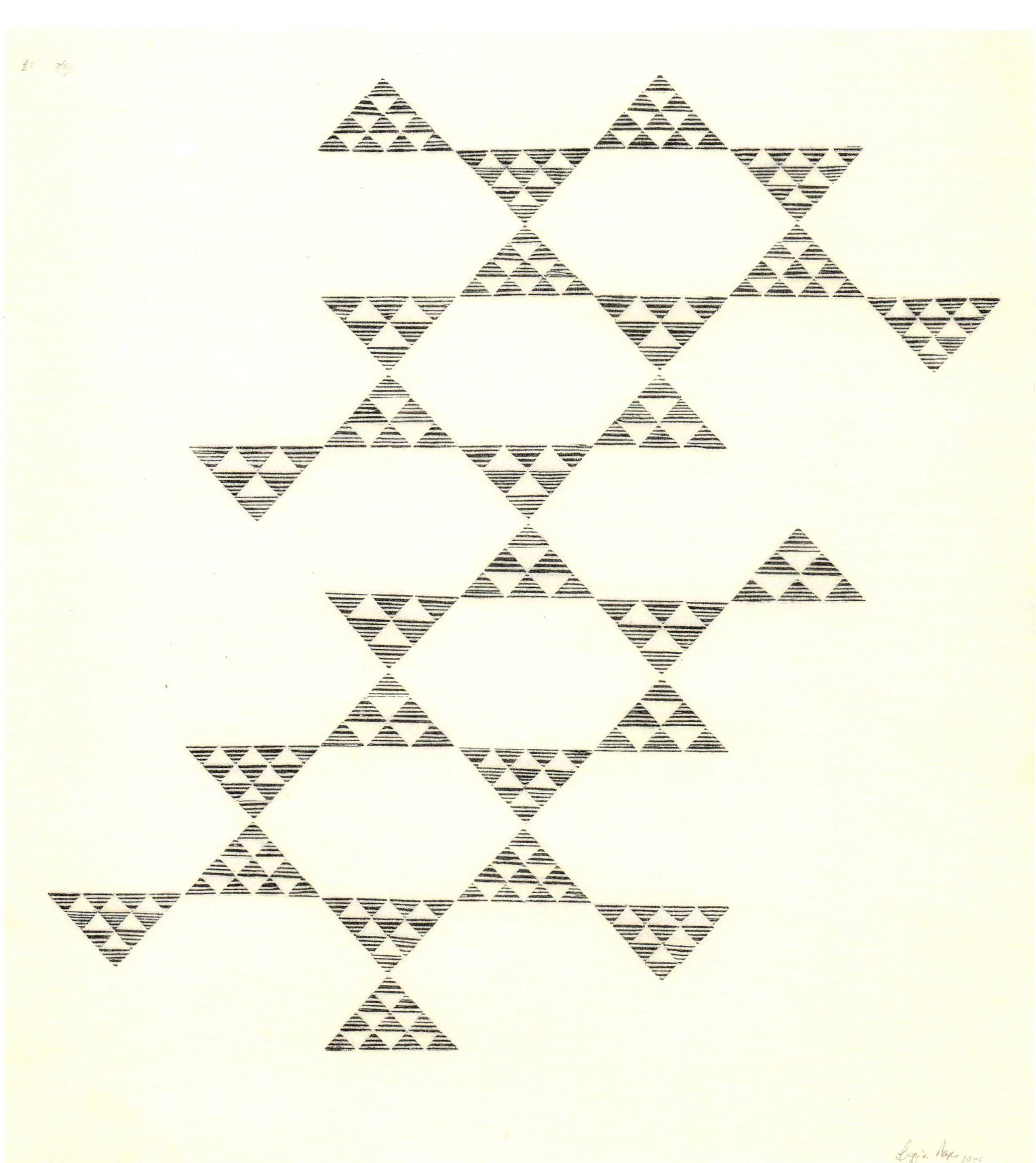

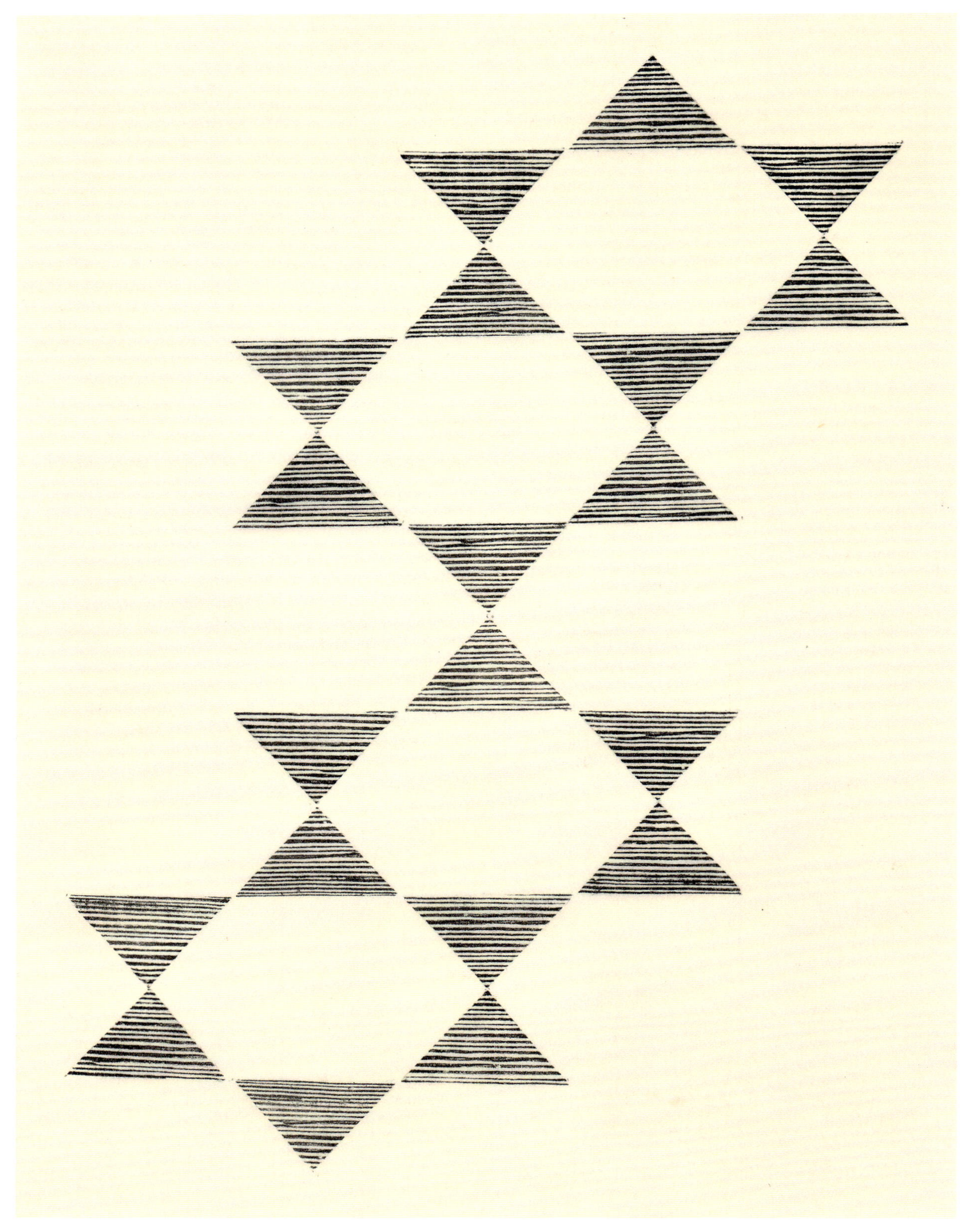

Tecelar, 1955

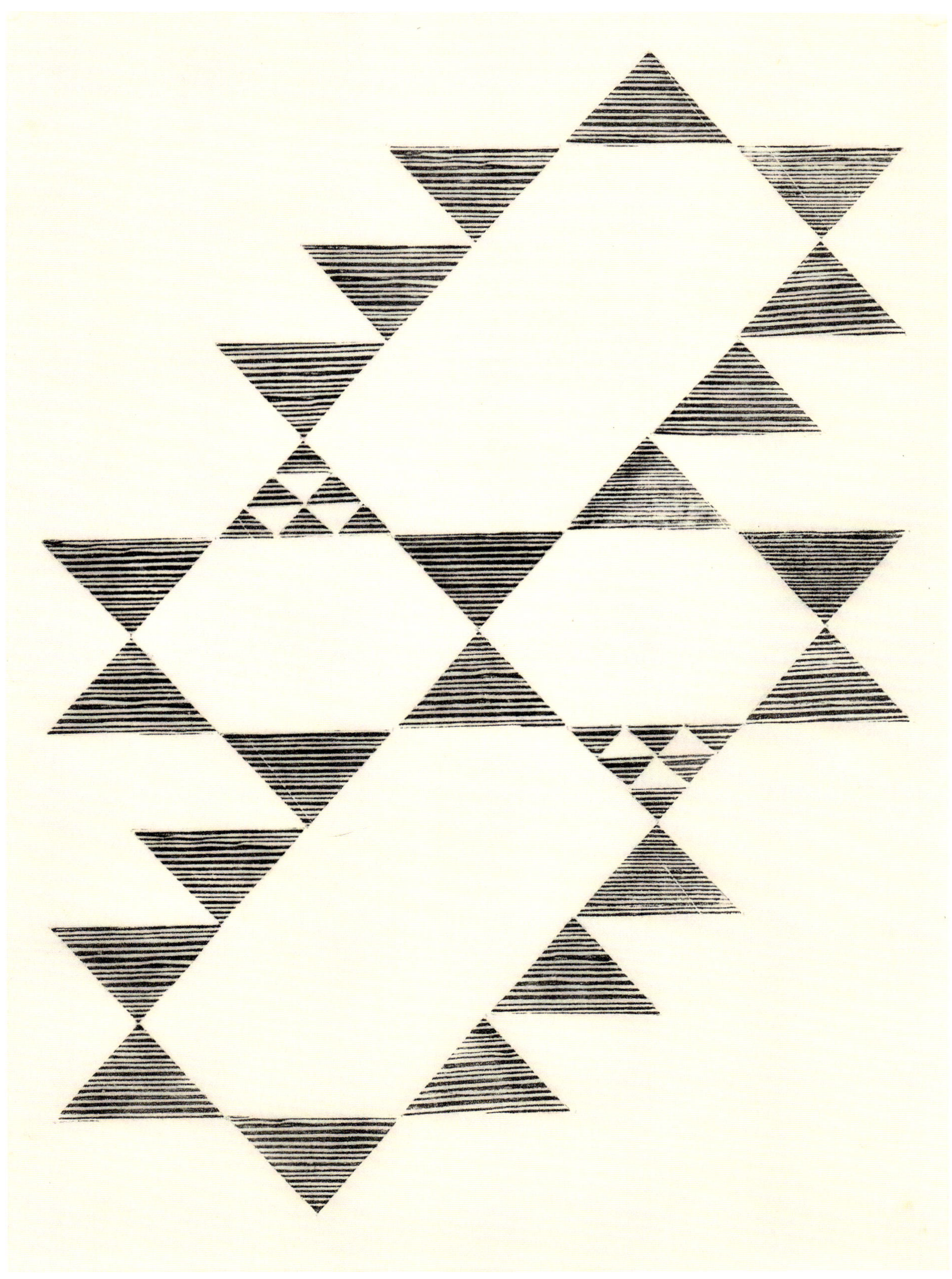

Tecelar, 1955

Tecelar, 1958

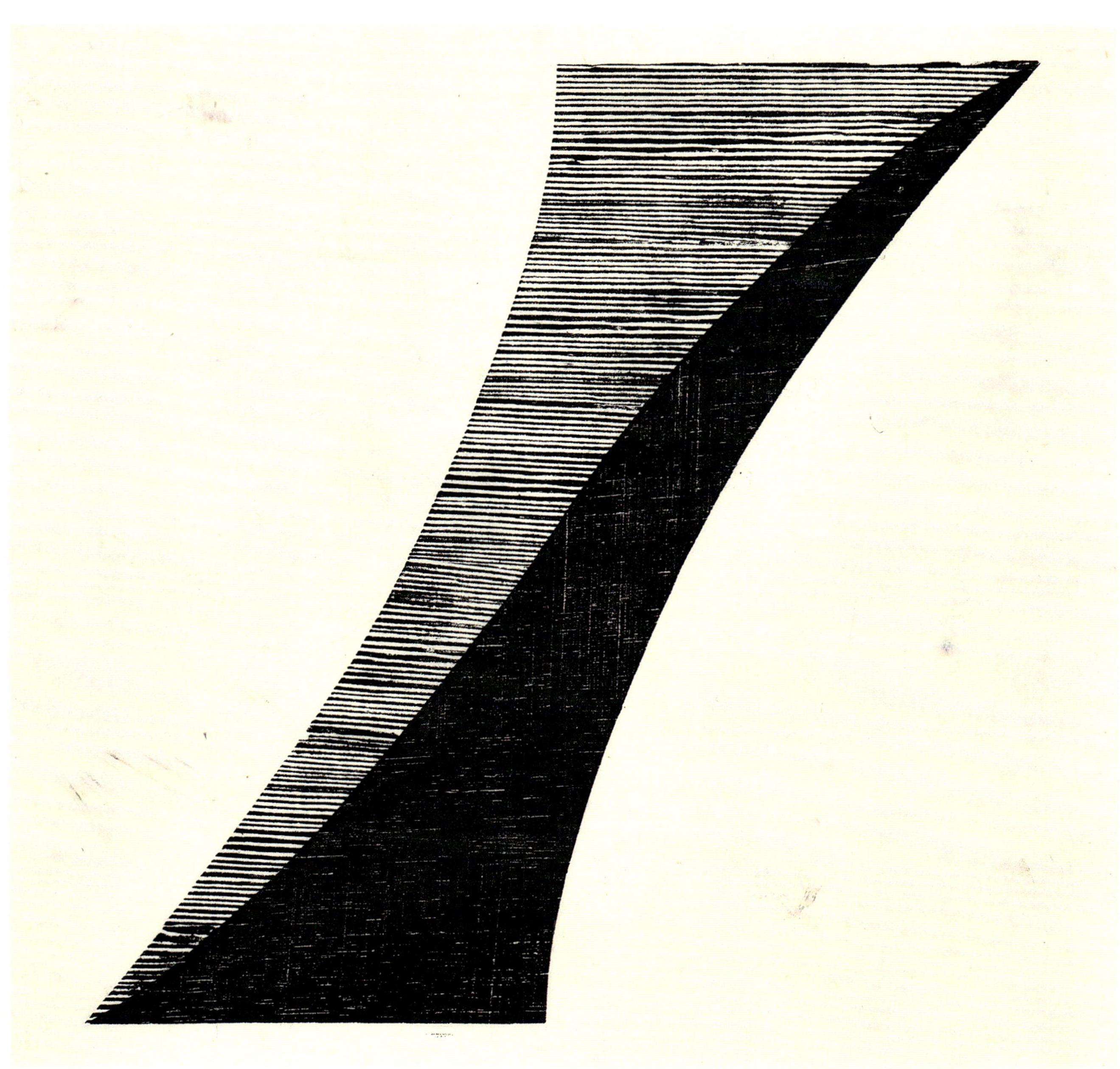

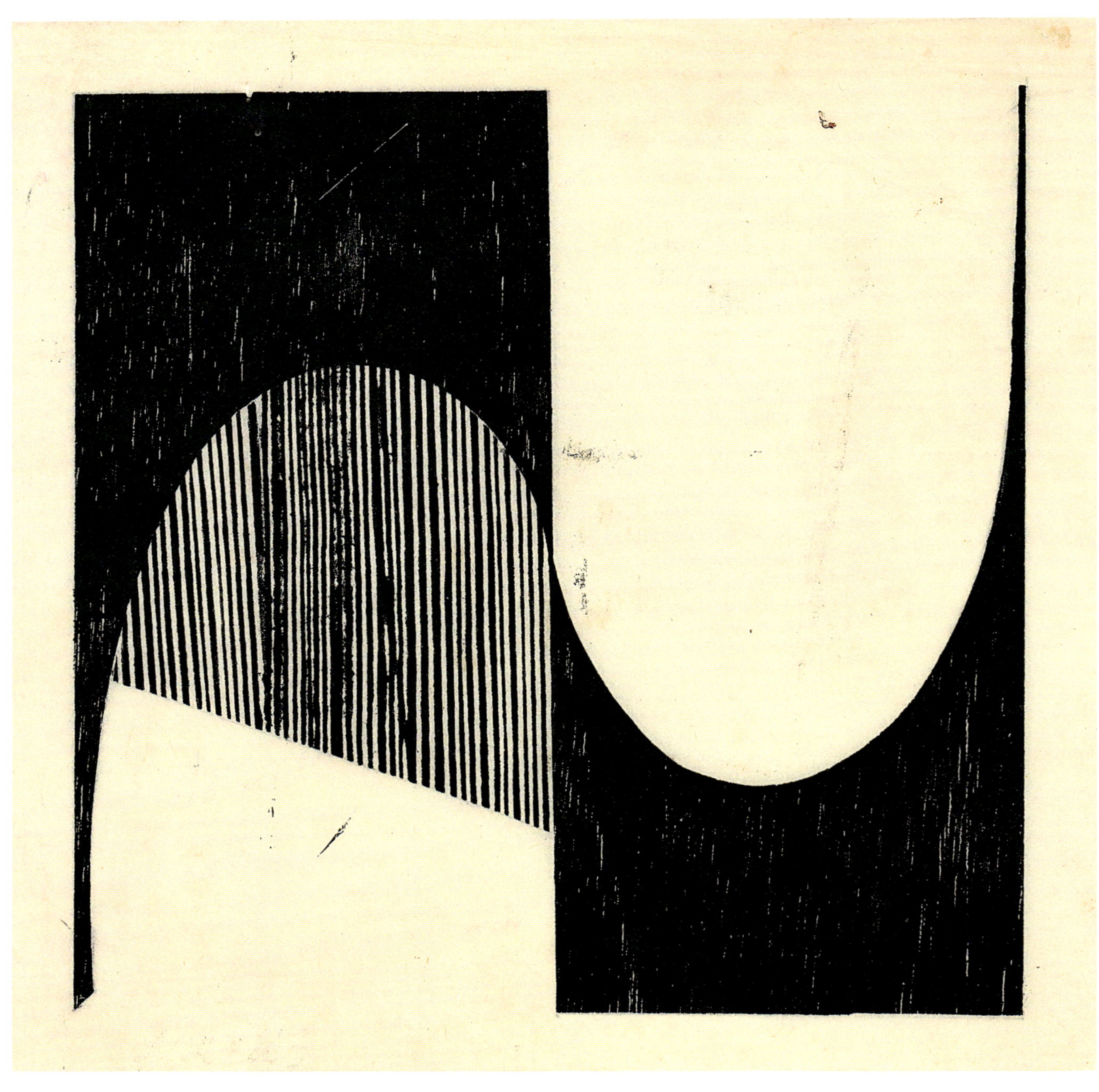

Tecelar, 1959

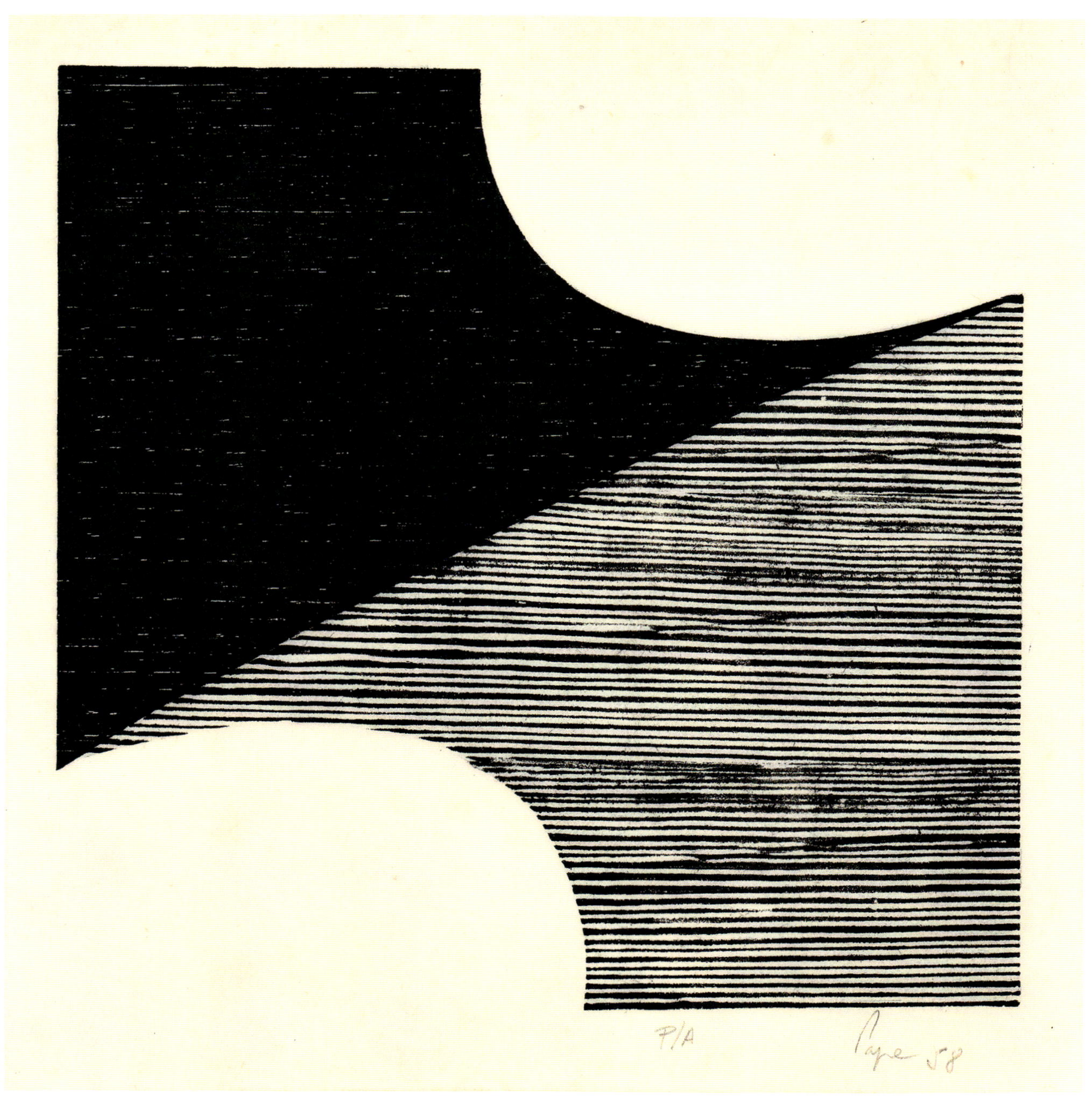

Tecelar, 1958

Desenho (Drawing), 1956

Nap 86

Desenho (Drawing), 1956

Soto
56

Desenho (Drawing), 1956

Desenho (Drawing), 1956

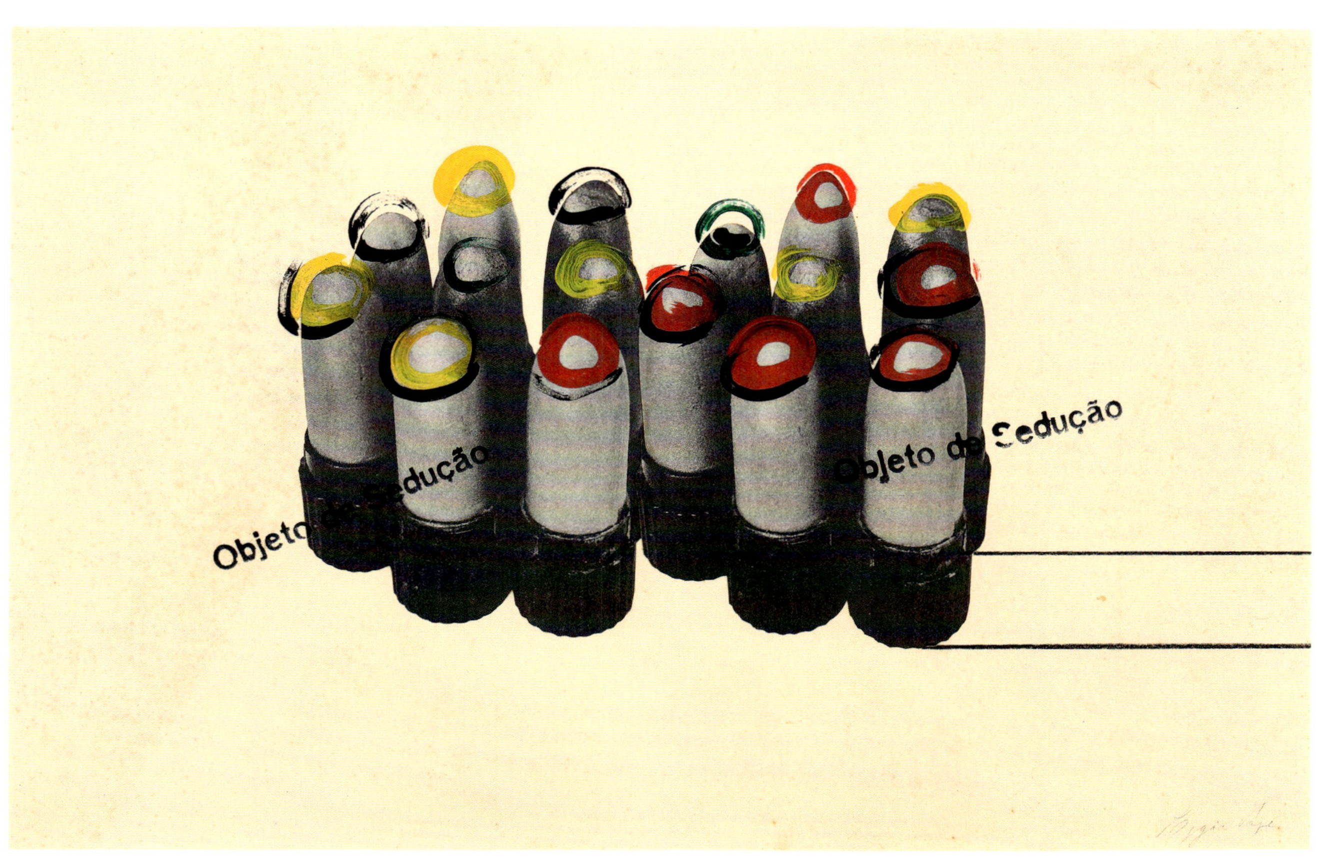

Objeto de Sedução (Object of Seduction), 1970

Objeto de Sedução (Object of Seduction), 1970

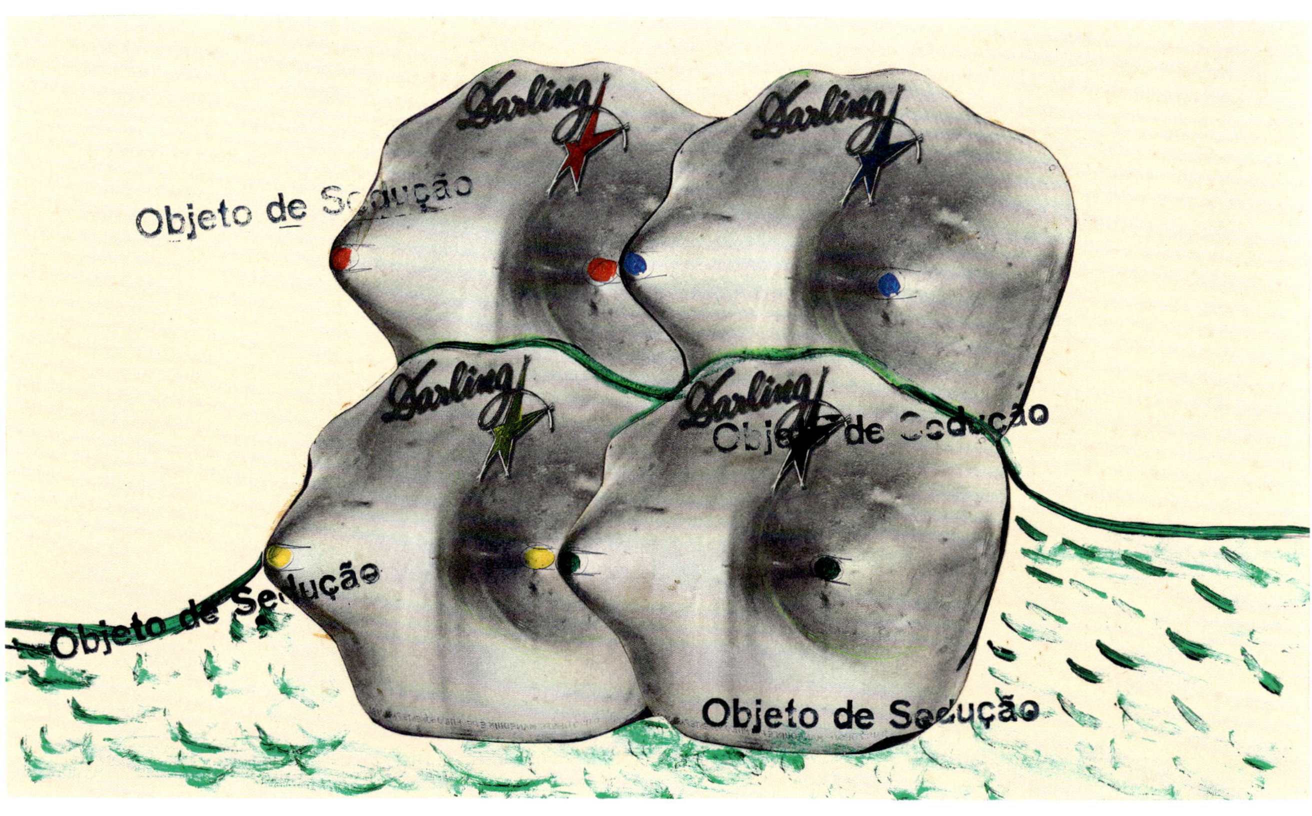
Objeto de Sedução
Darling
Darling
Darling
Darling
Objeto de Sedução
Objeto de Sedução
Objeto de Sedução

Untitled collage by Lygia Pape and Ivan Serpa, 1972

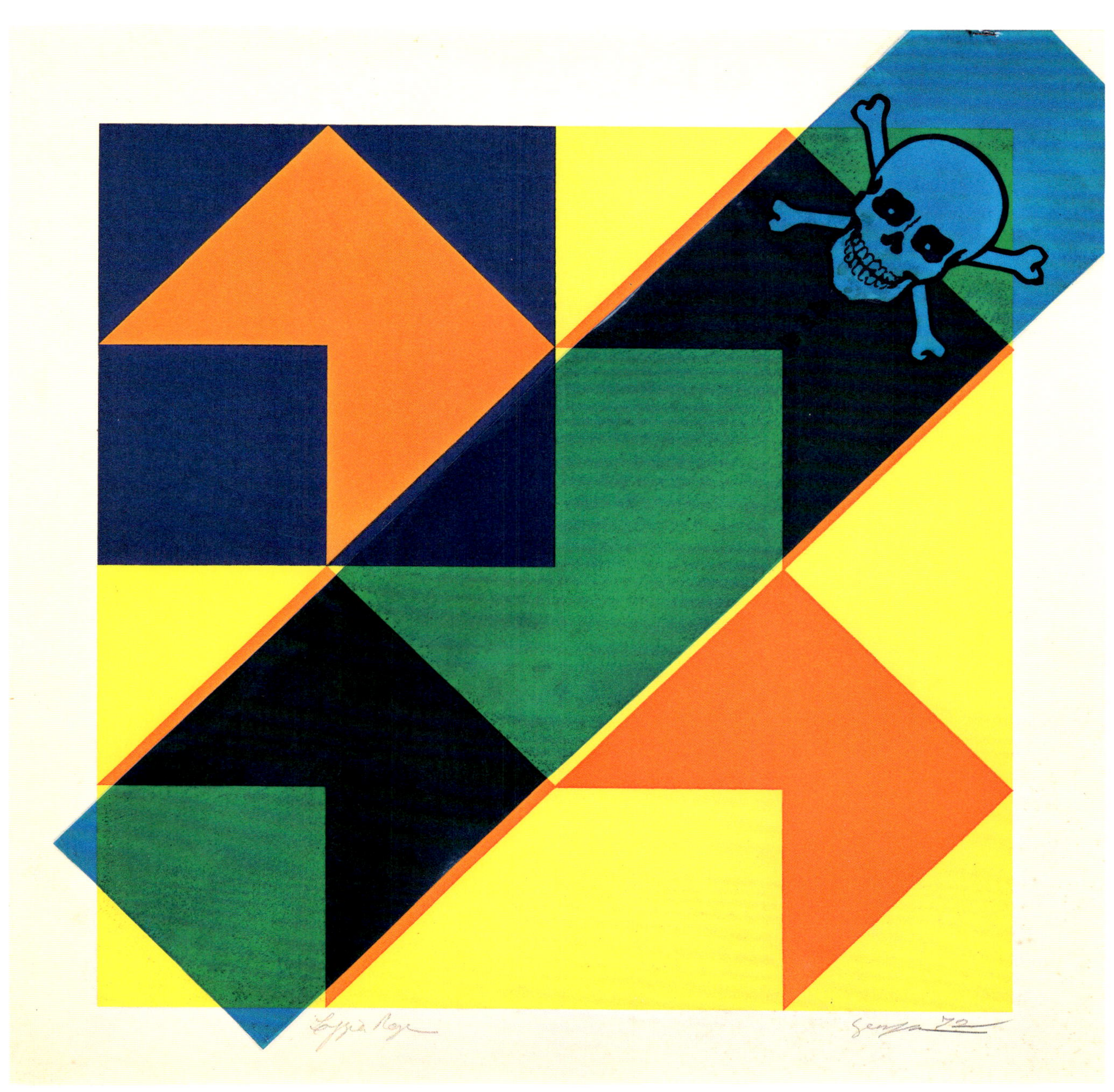

Untitled collage by Lygia Pape and Ivan Serpa, 1972

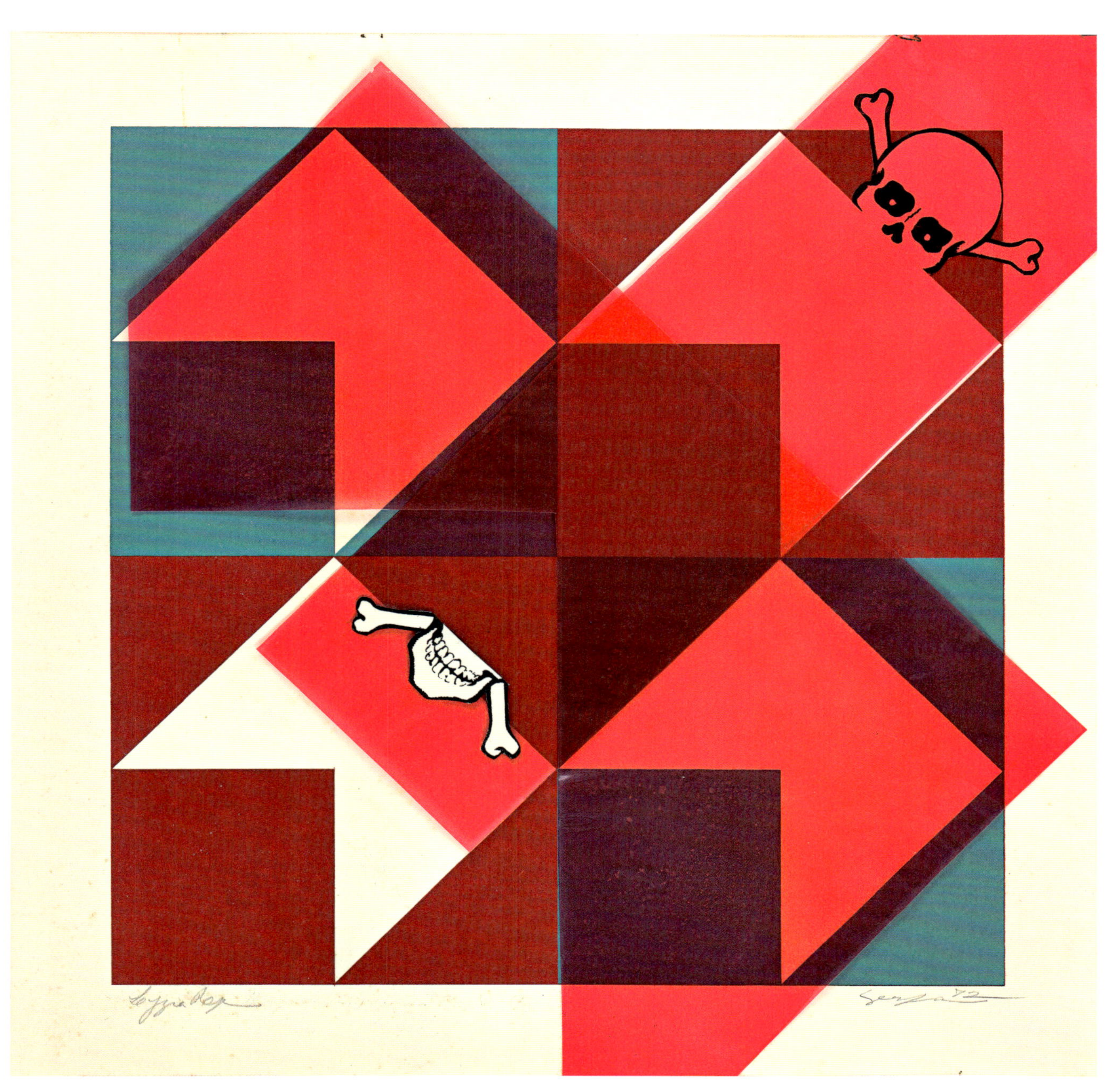

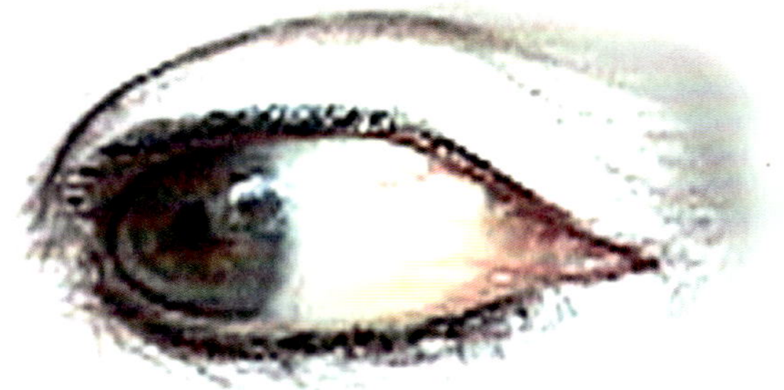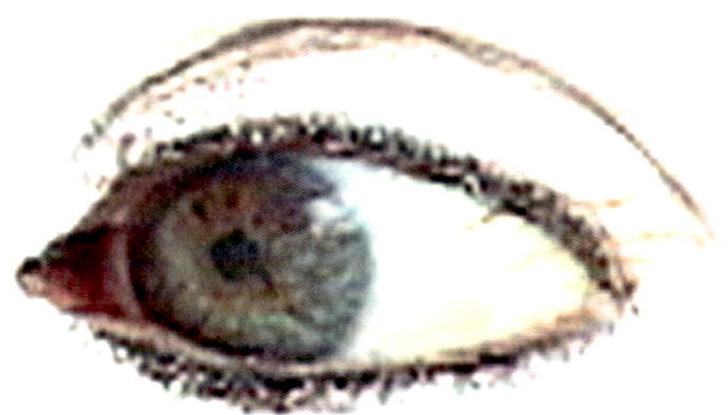

Jogo de Ténis (Tennis Game), 2001

The moving eyes of the *Tennis Game* installation stand in opposition to the fluidity of the *Books* circuit. In *Books* we are in direct contact with constructive works. In *Tennis Game*, the electronic image of a pair of eyes projected onto a large screen we are forced to view from a distance of less than one meter reinforces the unnatural nature of the mechanized image. Eyes that supposedly follow the movement of an invisible tennis ball, the sound of which is stridently metallic, move like a metronome in their absolute regularity. We do not merely look at them—we are actually inside these machine-eyes. I recall an ad in the trolley cars of my childhood. The image of a pair of eyes (judging from the eyelashes they were women's eyes) and the phrase: "Just as you see me, all the ads on this trolley car are seen." In those days, it was enough for the virtual gaze to attract a real gaze. In this time of greater cynicism and more hardened defenses, the artist pushes us up against her eyes and mobilizes our bodies within the narrow corridor of a tennis game in which there is neither tennis court nor a ball, let alone players, in an intelligent inversion of the finale of Antonioni's *Blow Up*.

—Paulo Sergio Duarte, "Risco e invenção," translated as "Risk and Invention," in *Lygia Pape*, exh. cat. (Rio de Janeiro: Centro de Arte Hélio Oiticica, 2002), pp. 68–69.

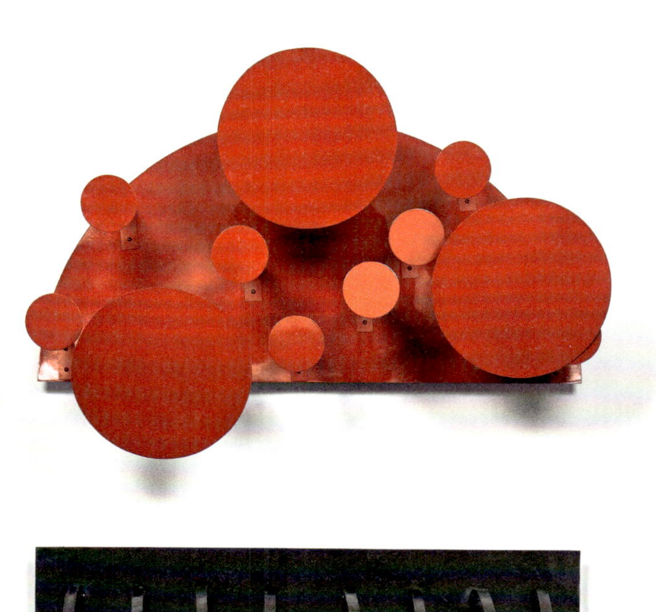
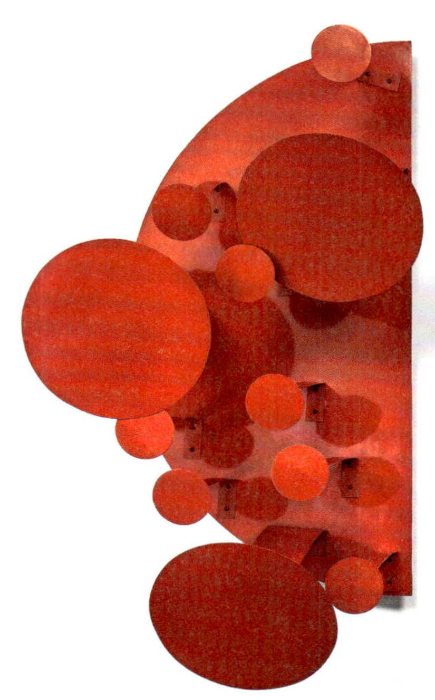
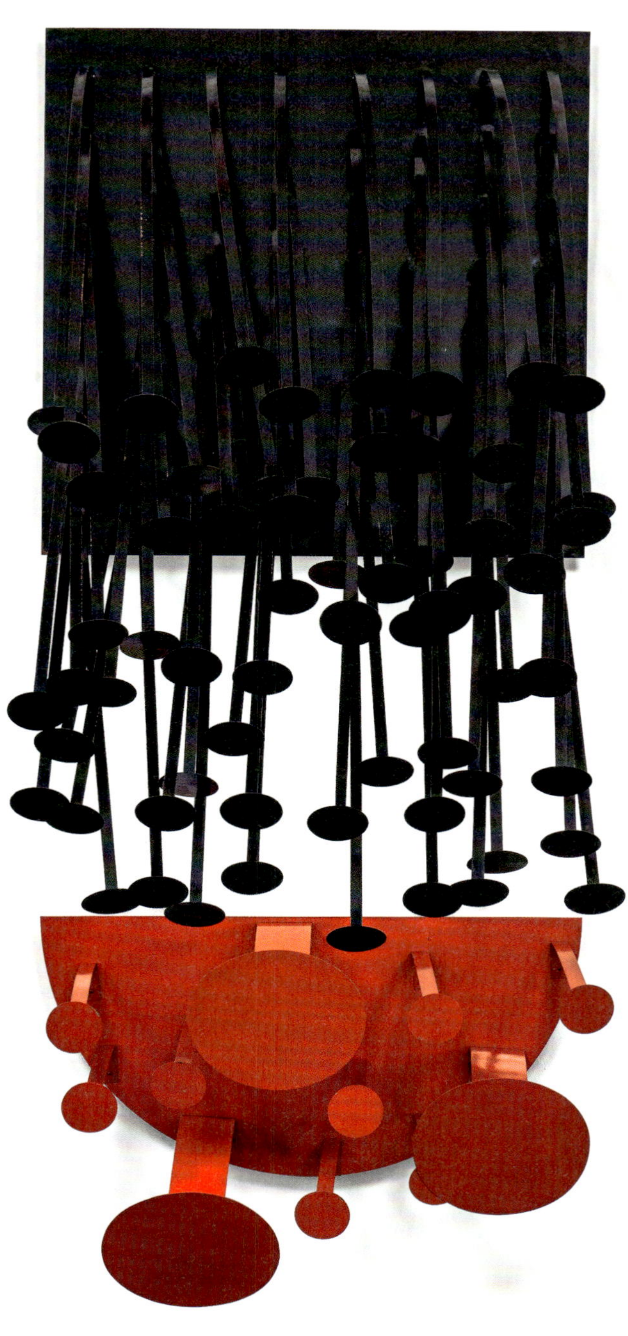
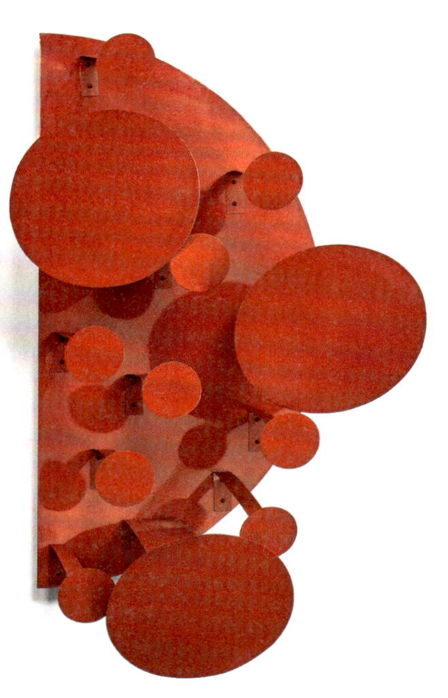
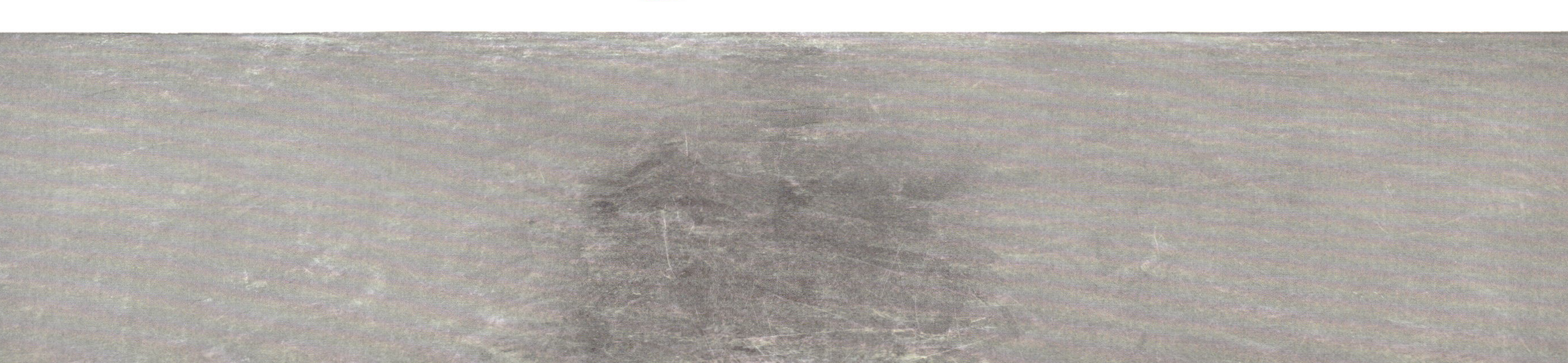

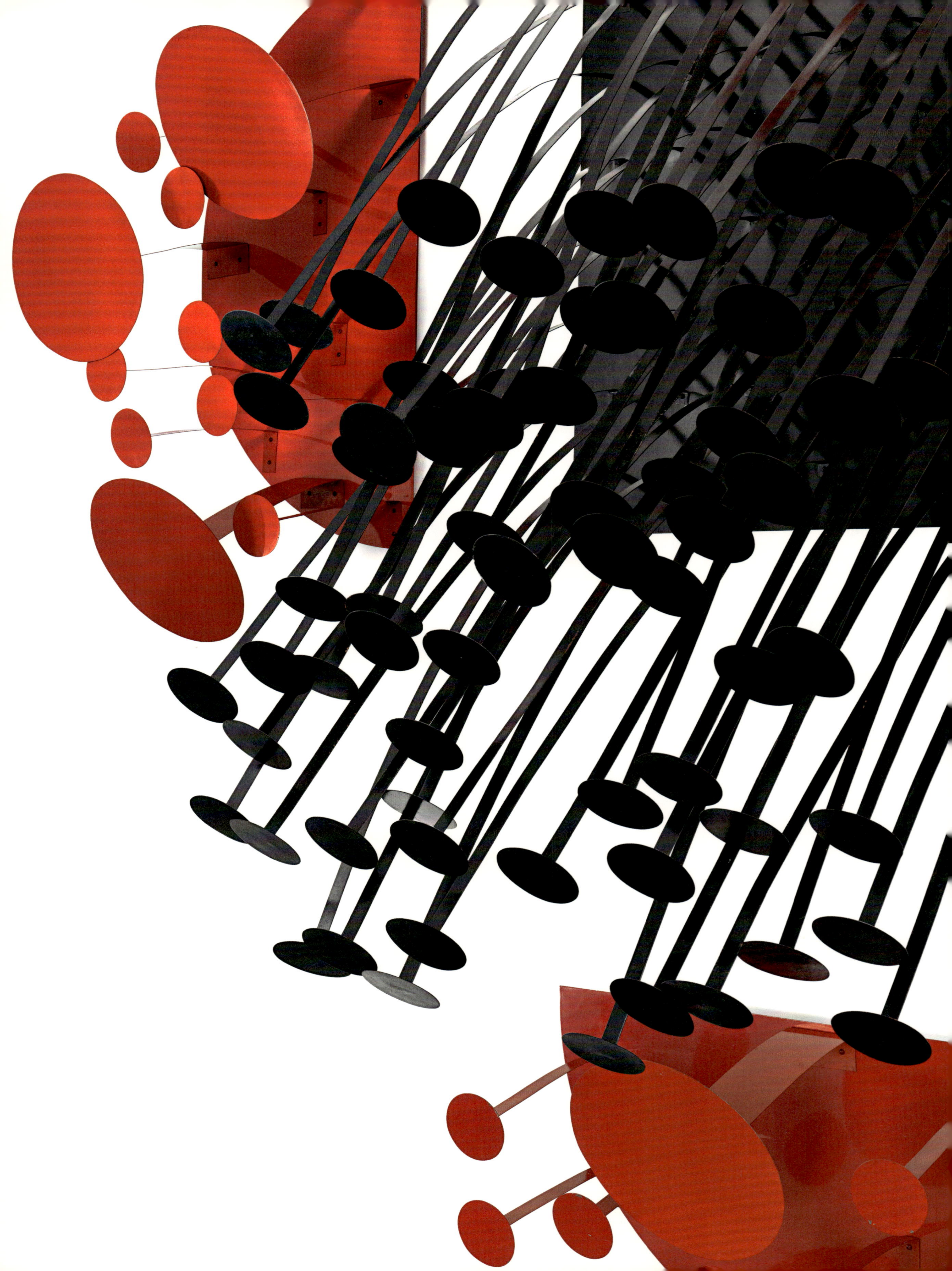

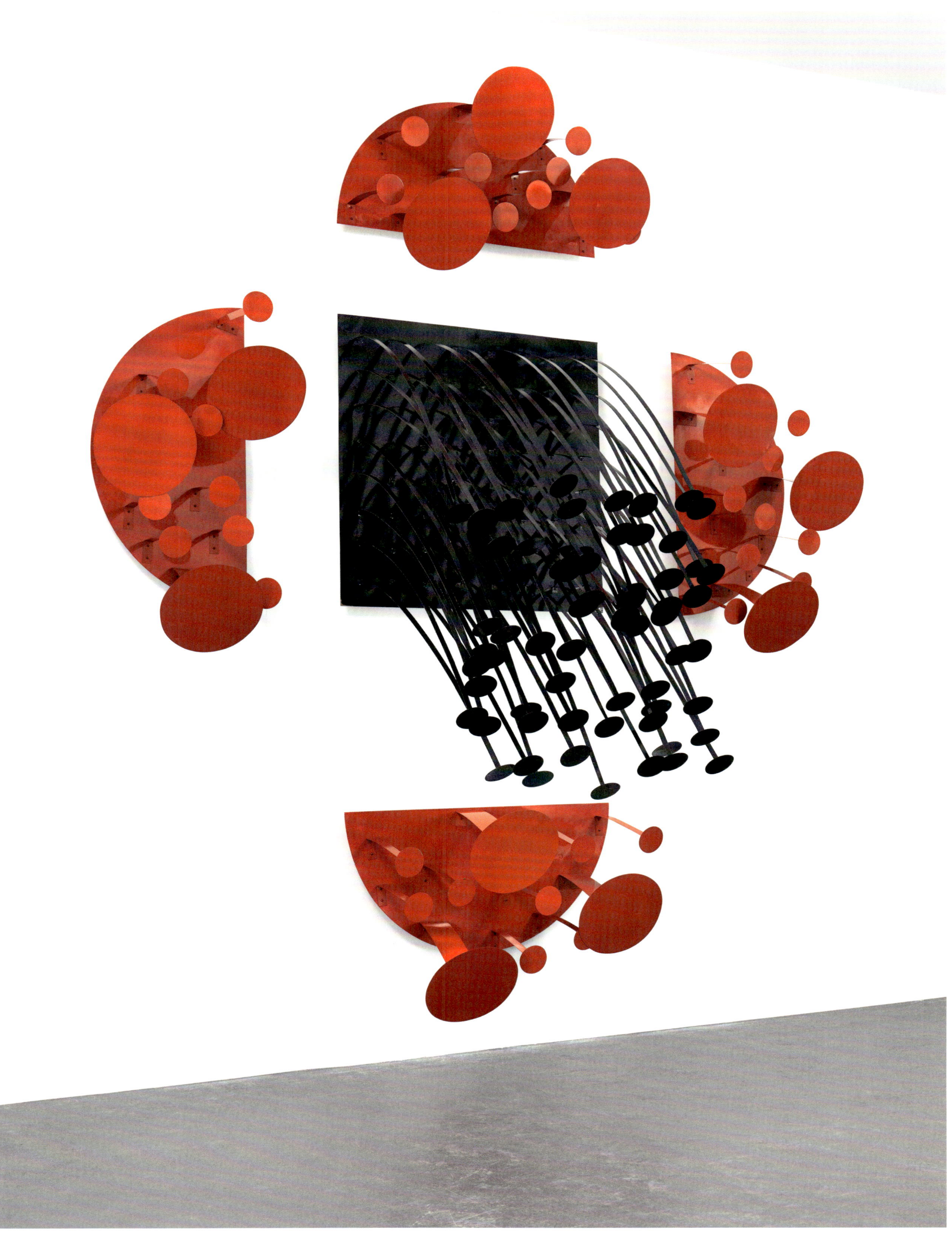

Amazonino Vermelho e Preto (Red and Black Amazonino), 1990

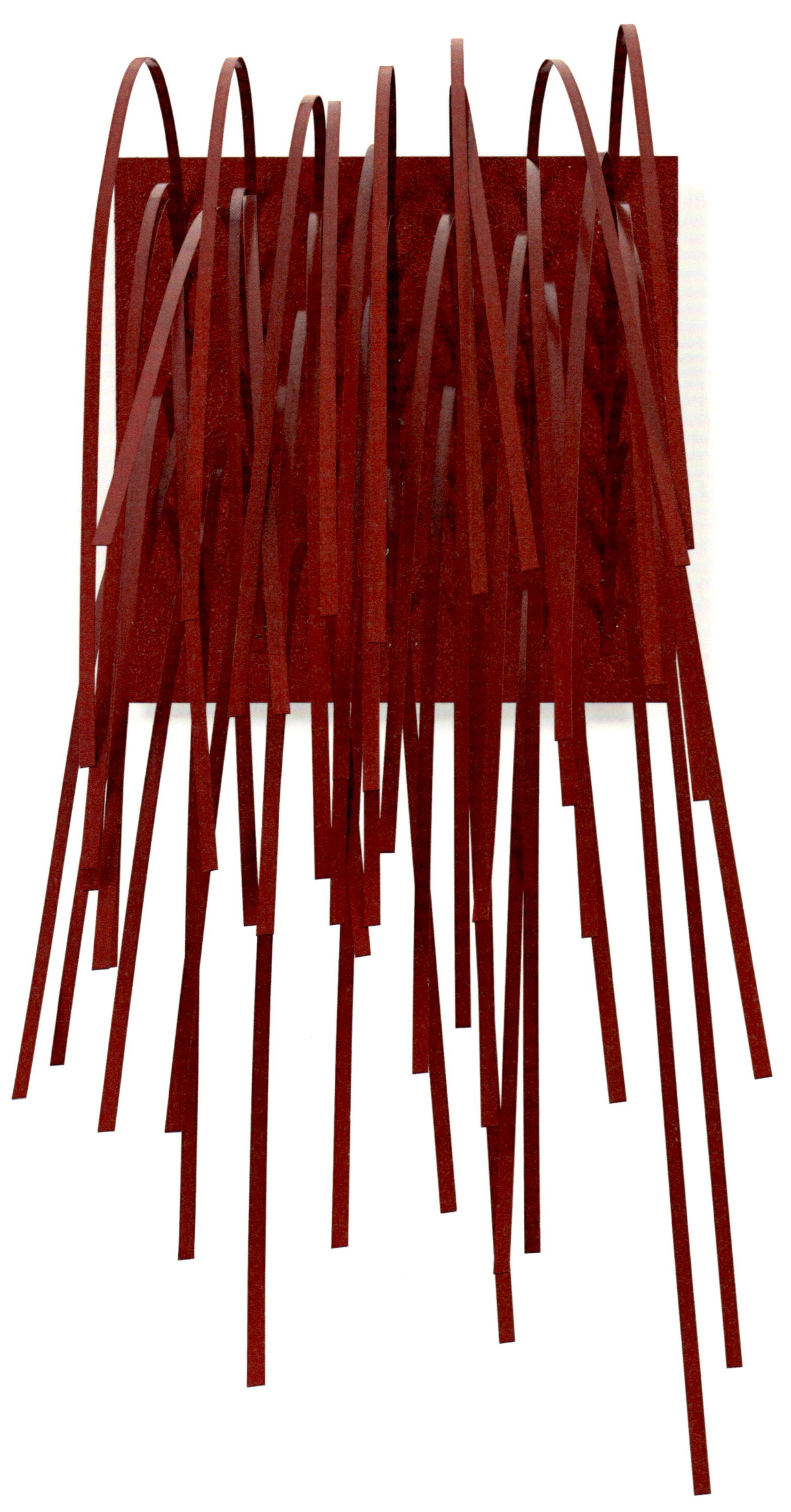

 Amazonino Vermelho (Red Amazonino), 1989/2003

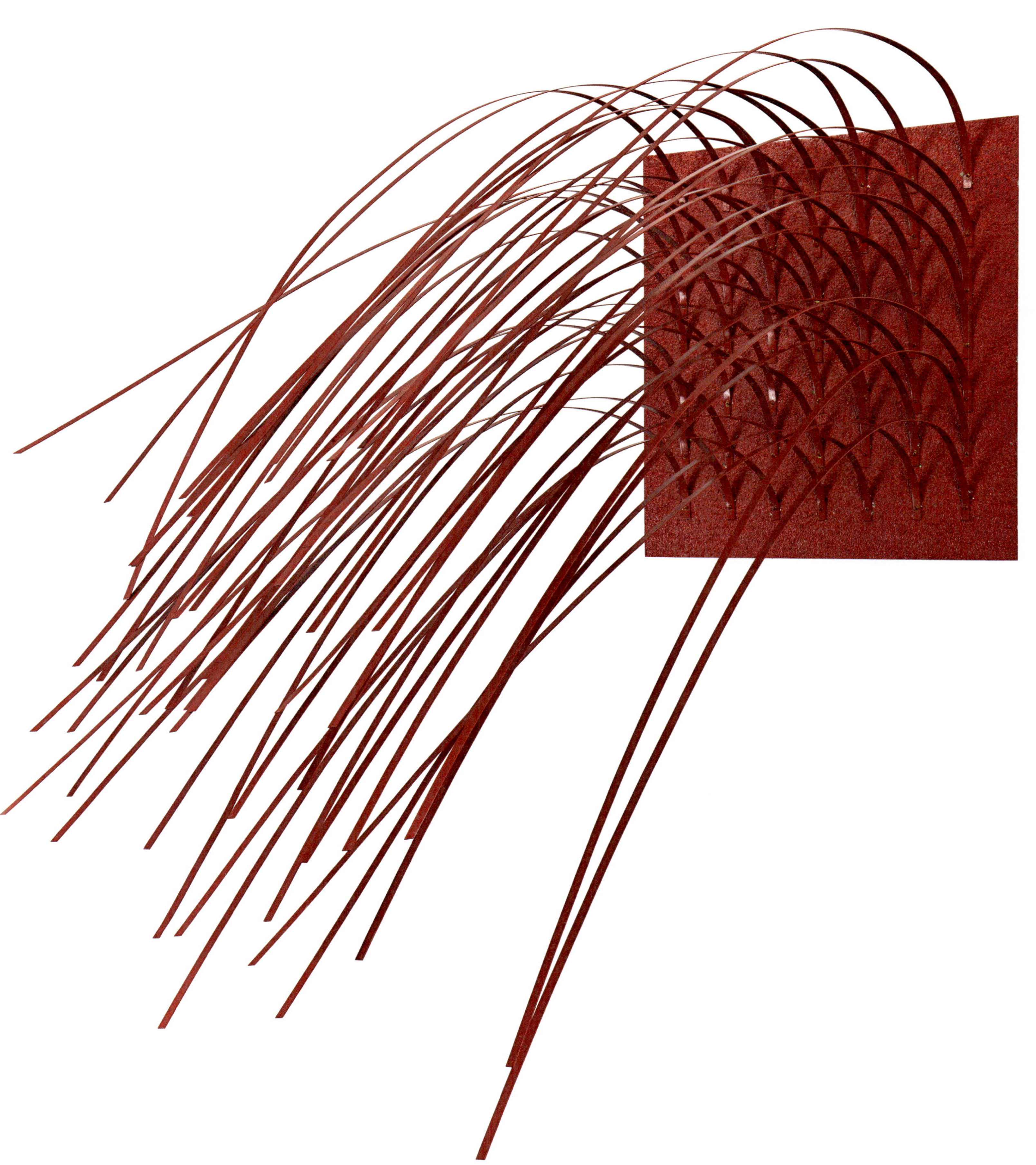

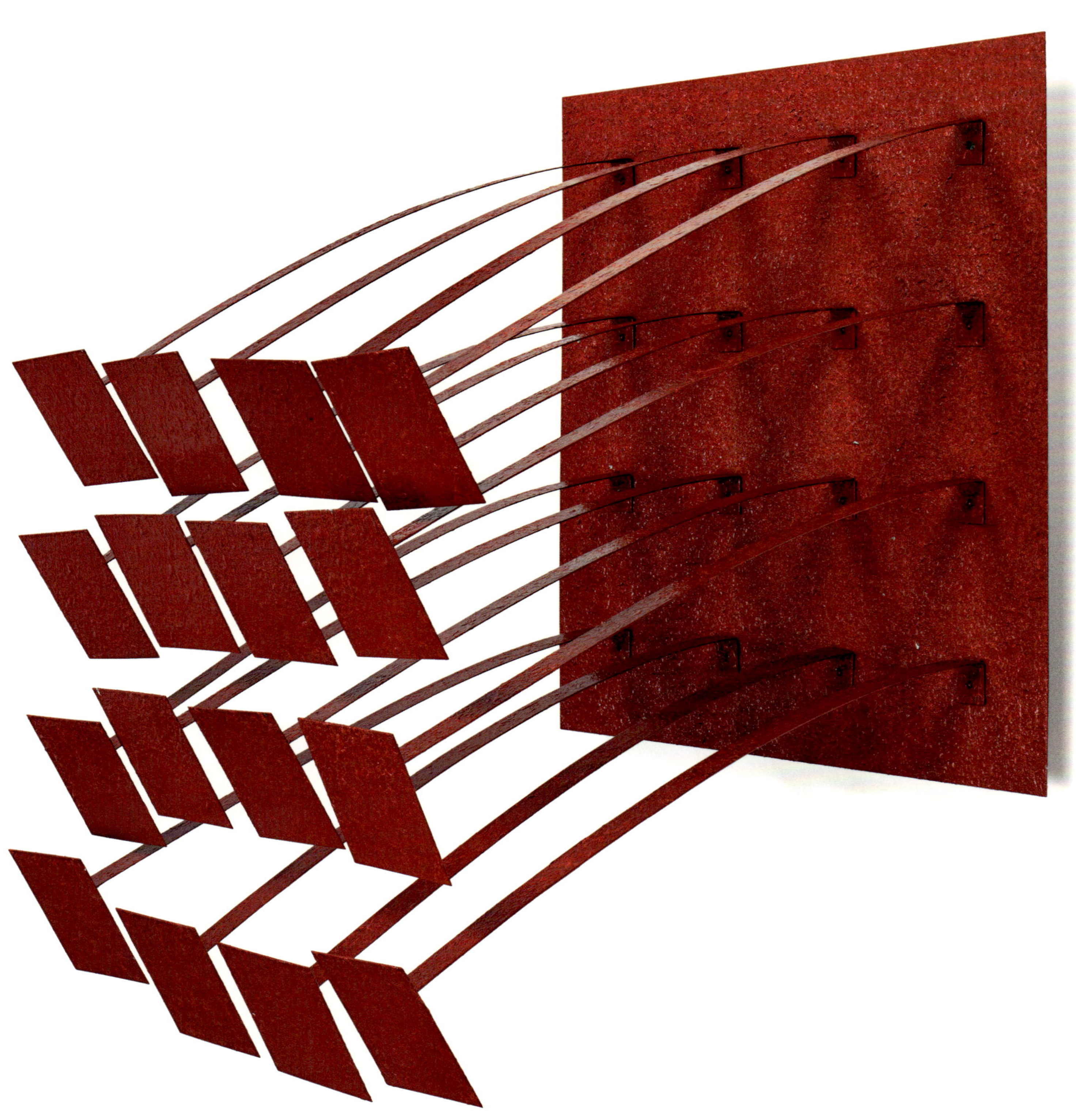

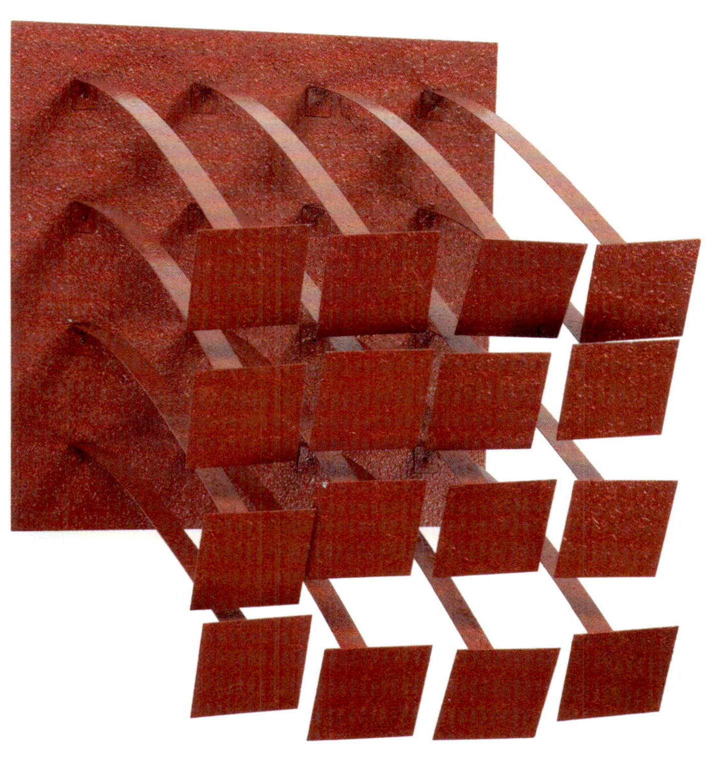

  Amazonino Vermelho (Red Amazonino), 1989/2003

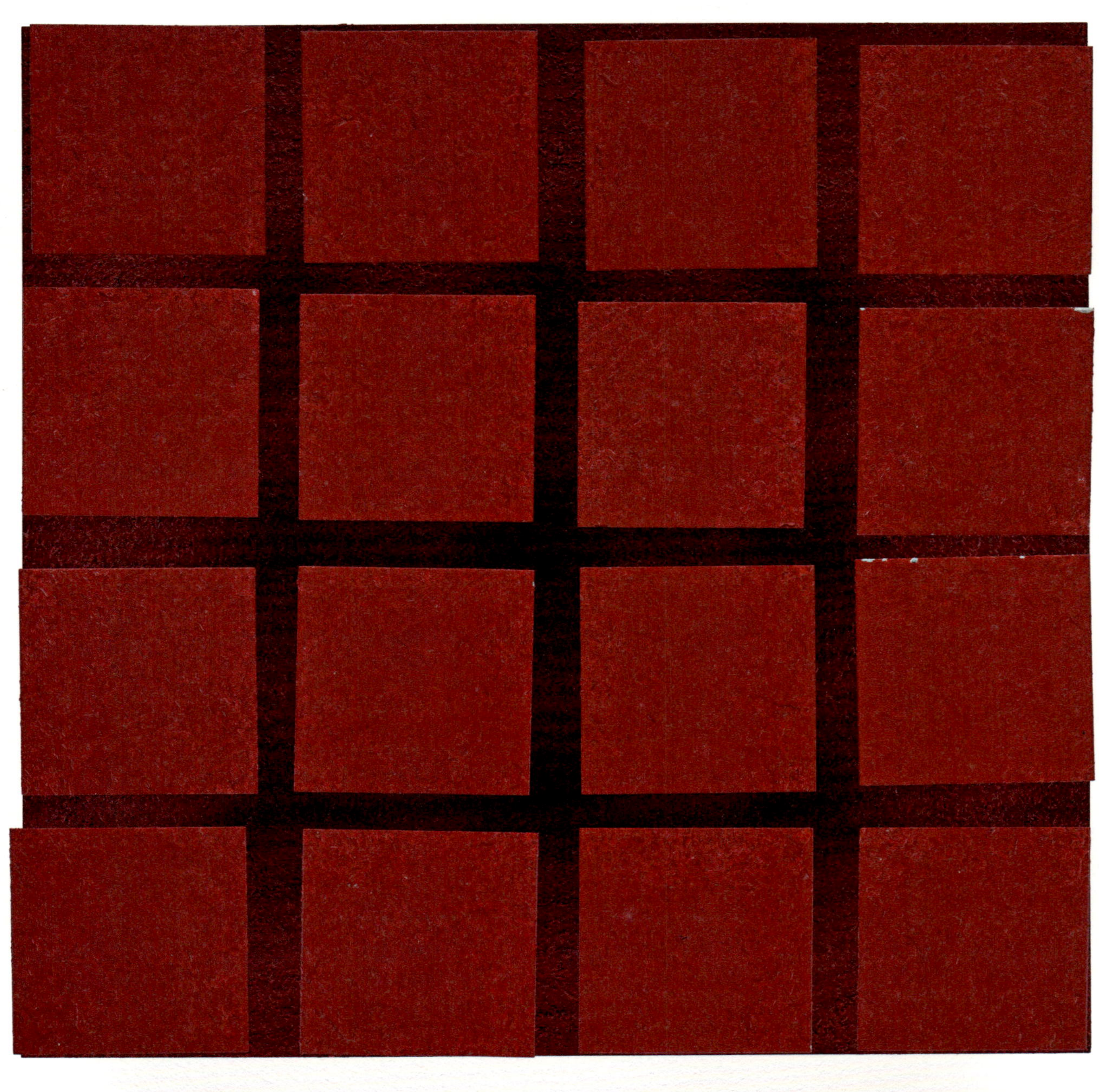

 Amazonino Vermelho (Red Amazonino), 1989/2003

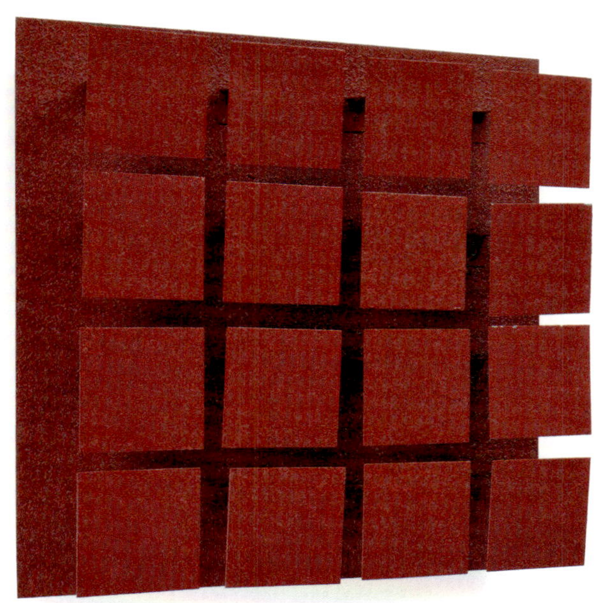

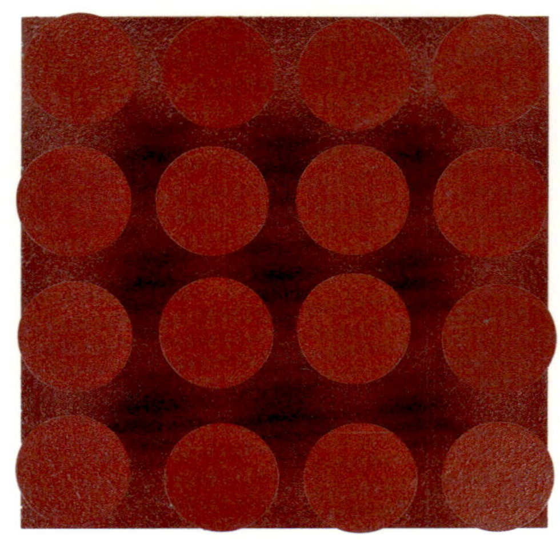

   Amazonino Vermelho (Red Amazonino), 1989/2003

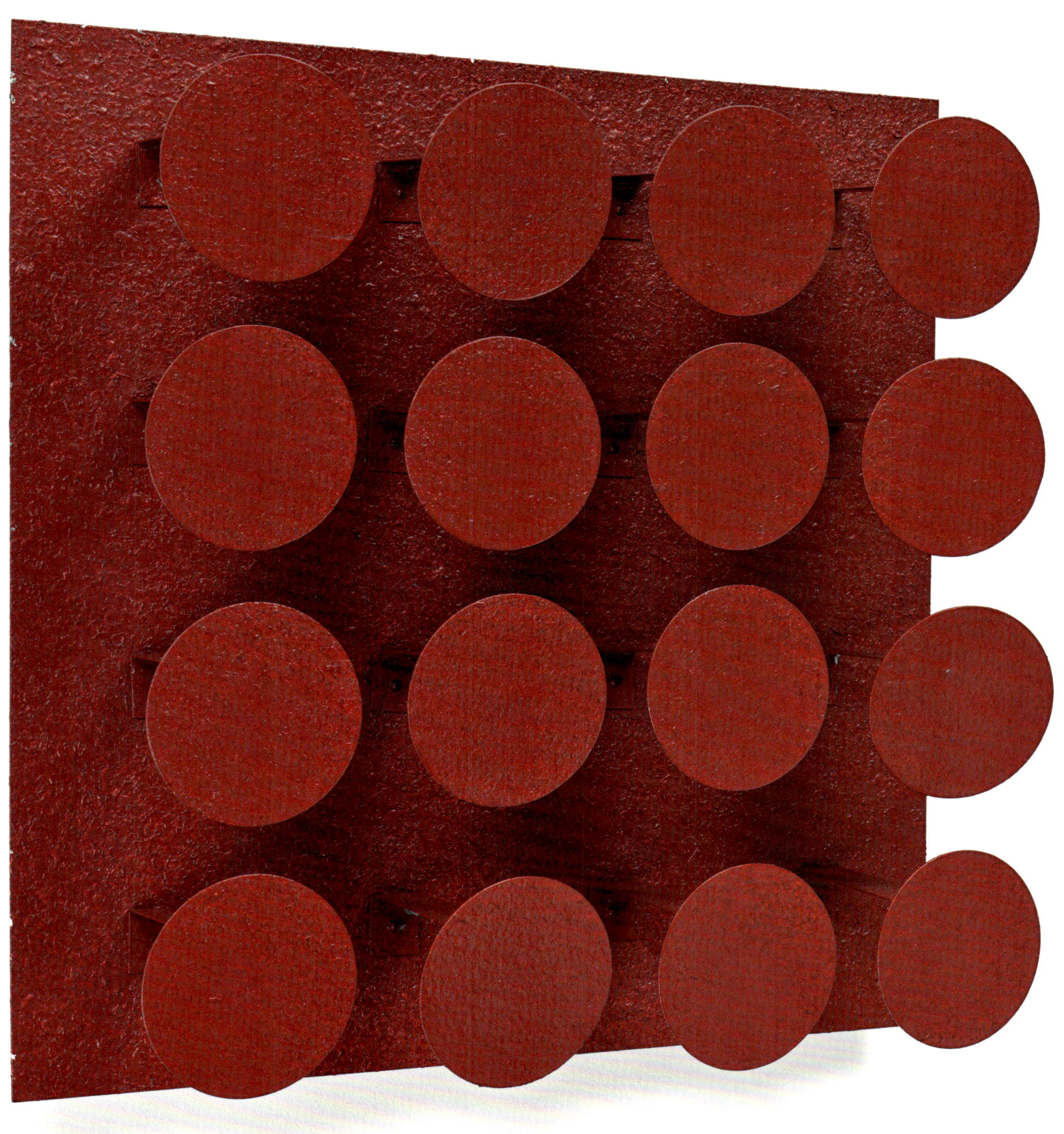

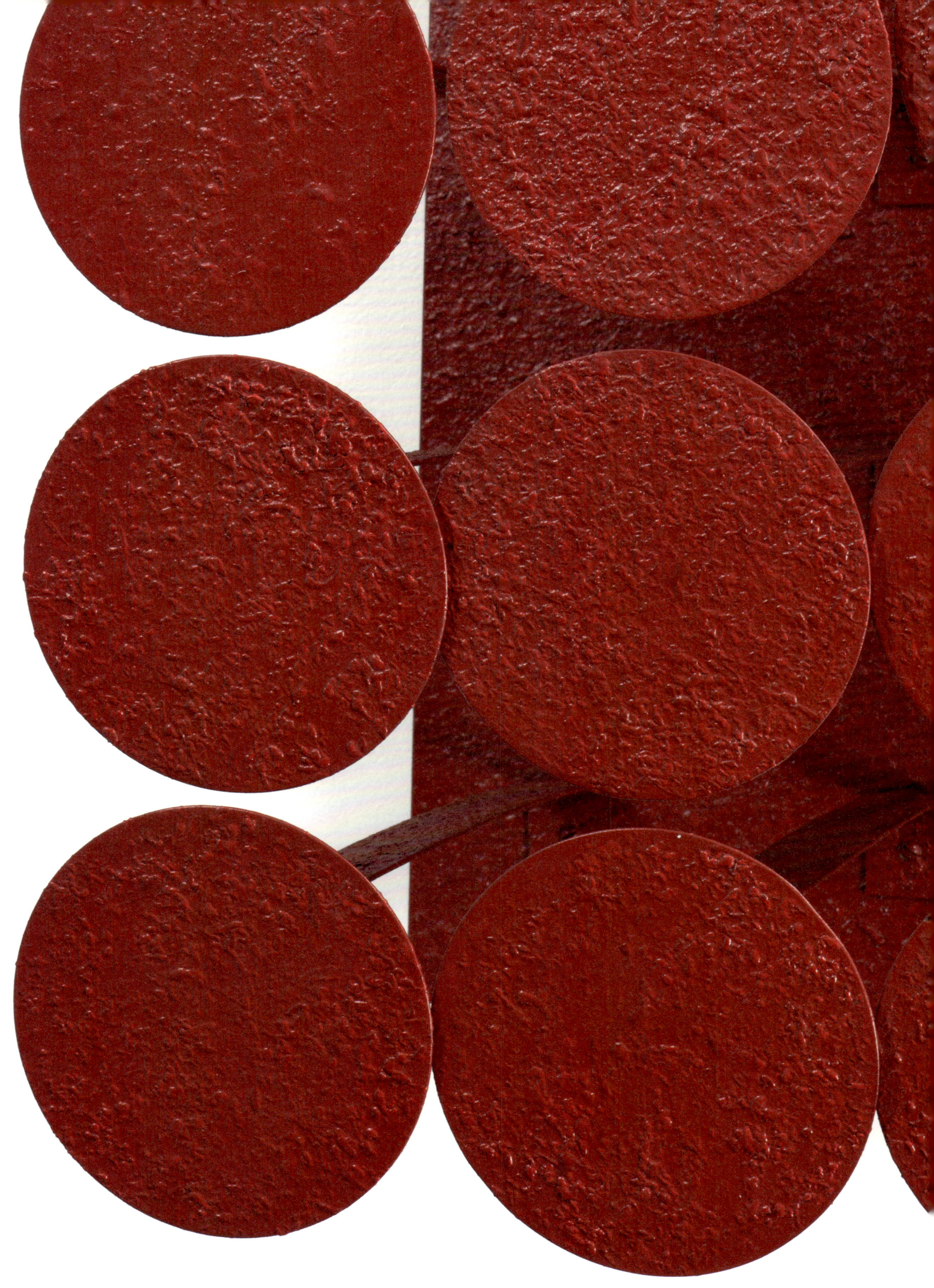

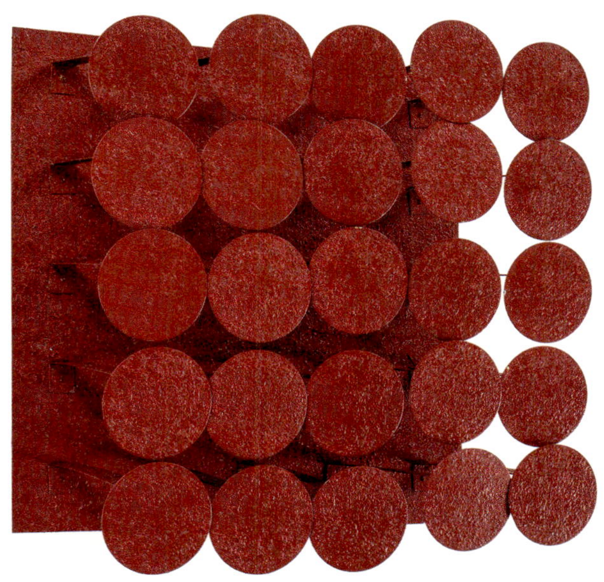

    Amazonino Vermelho (Red Amazonino), 1989/2003

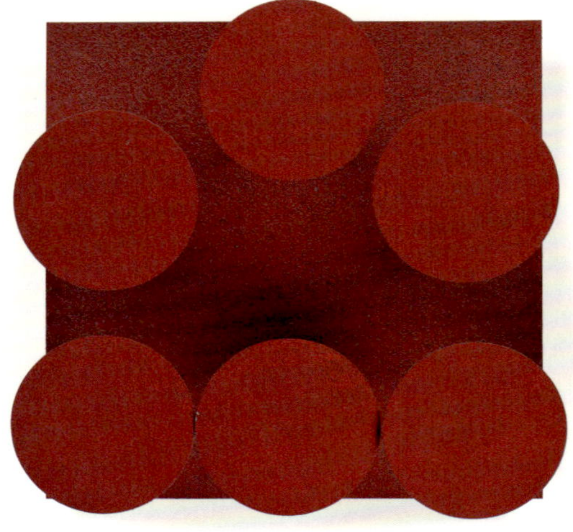

  Amazonino Vermelho (Red Amazonino), 1989/2003

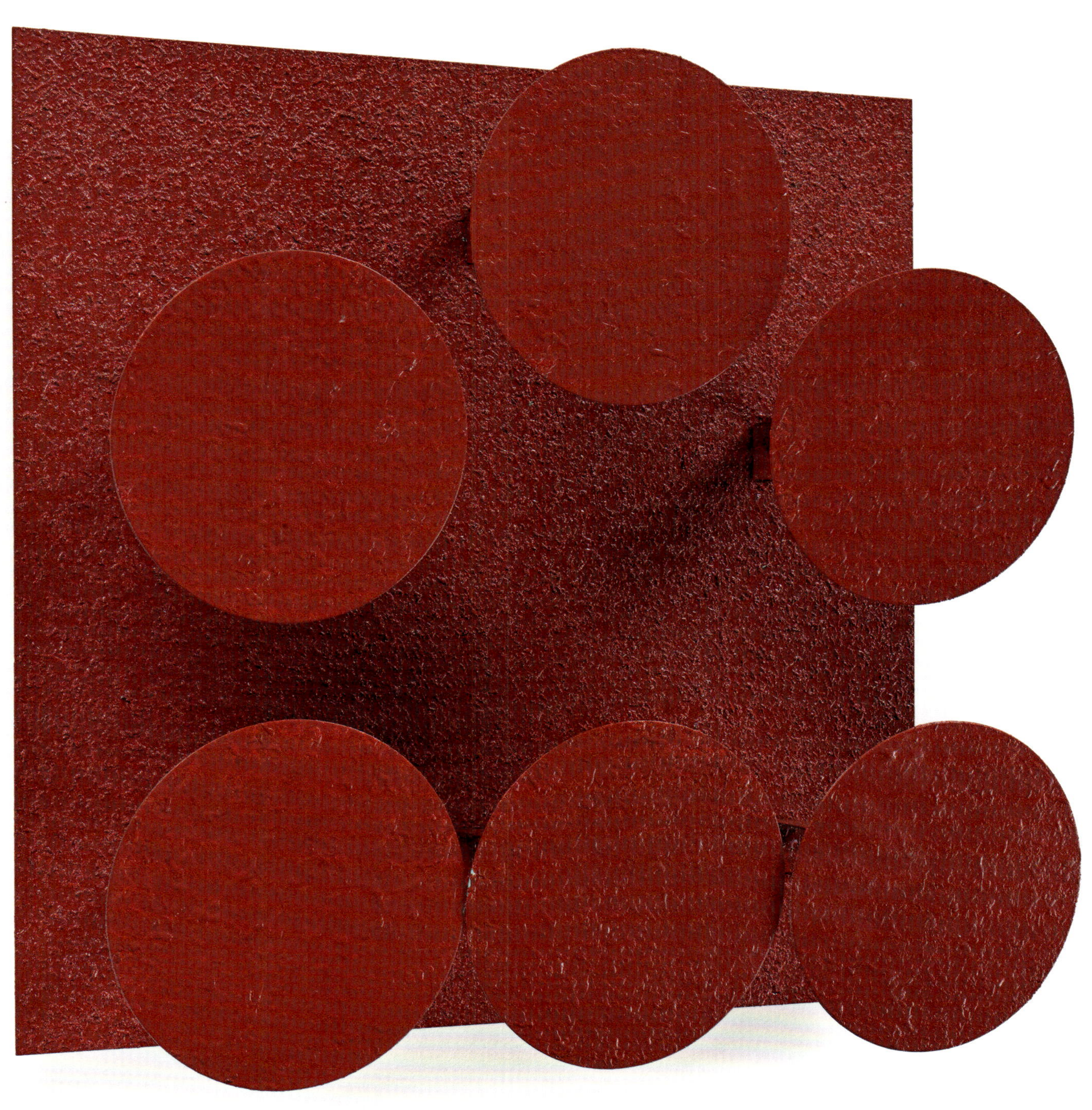

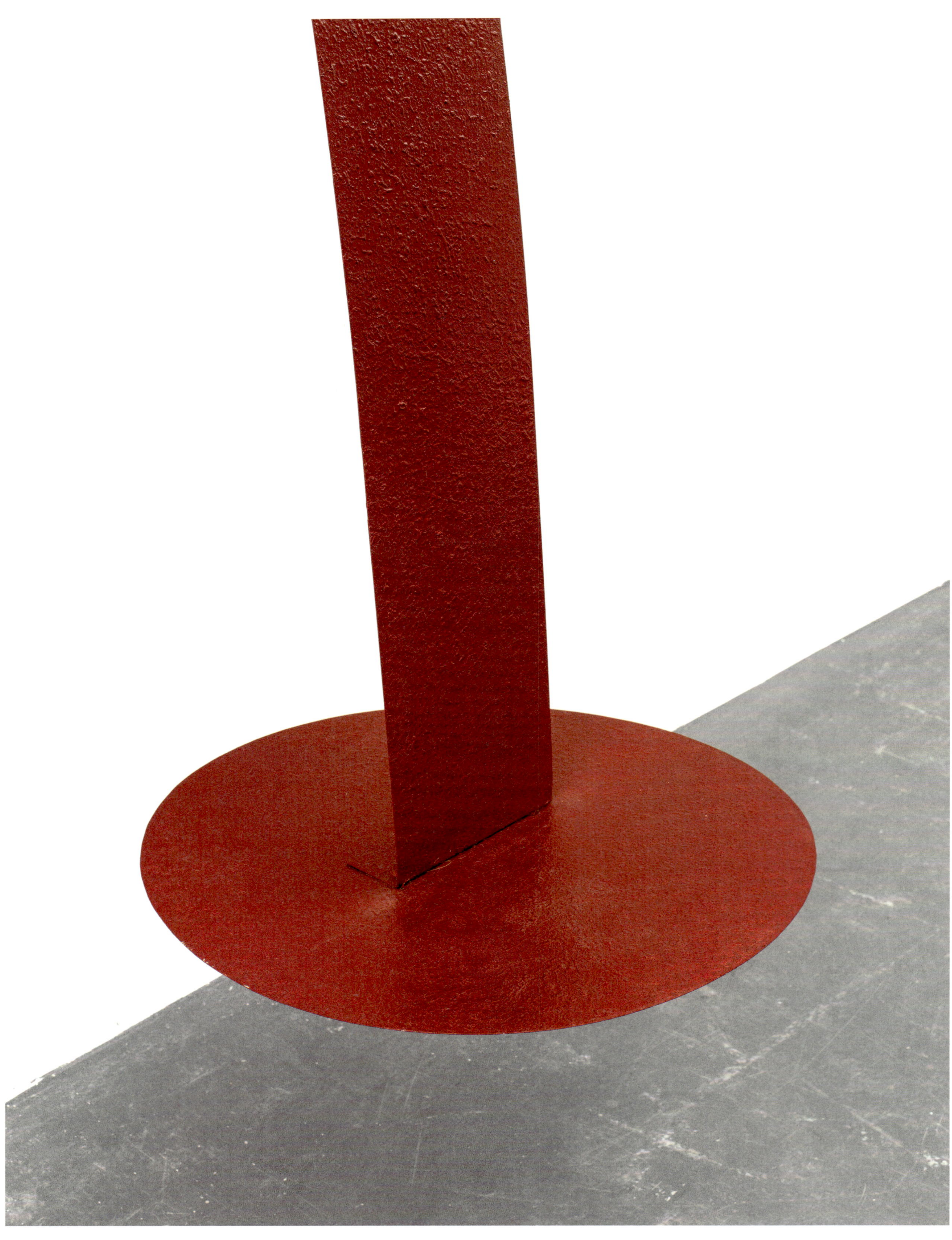

Amazonino Vermelho (Red Amazonino), 1989/2003

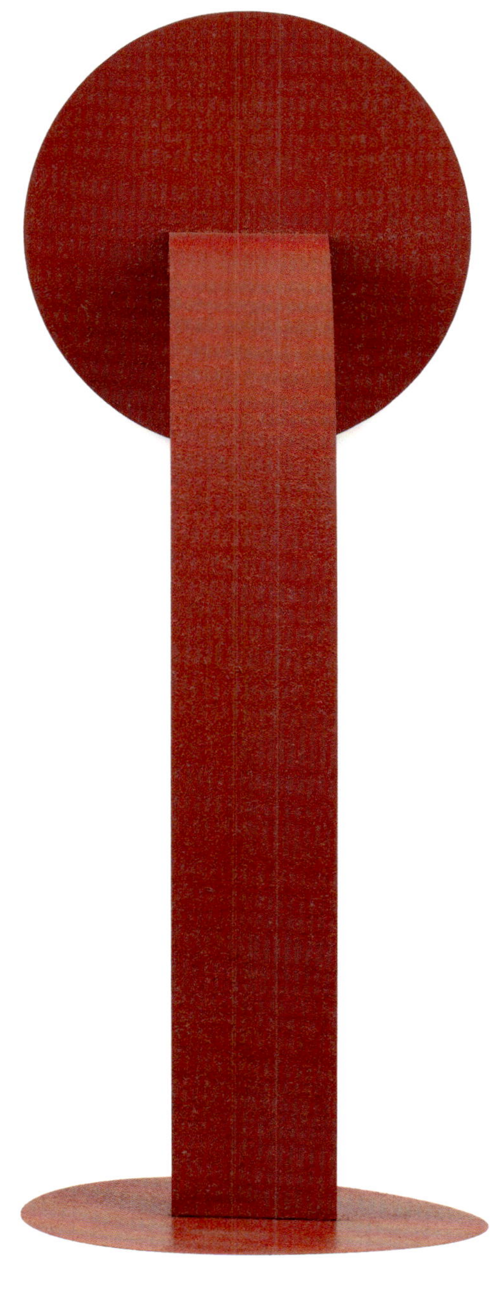

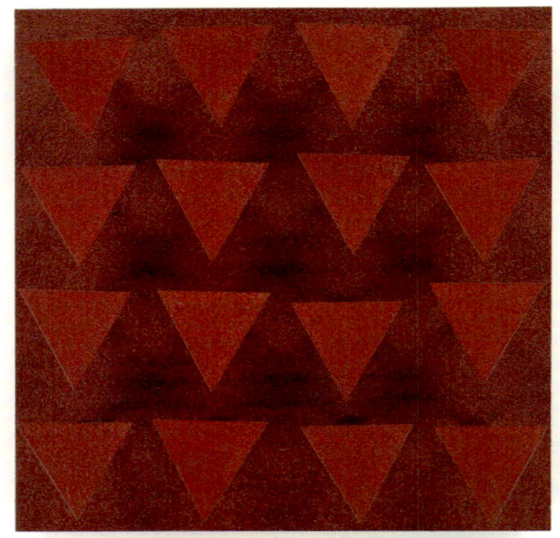

 Amazonino Vermelho (Red Amazonino), 1989/2003

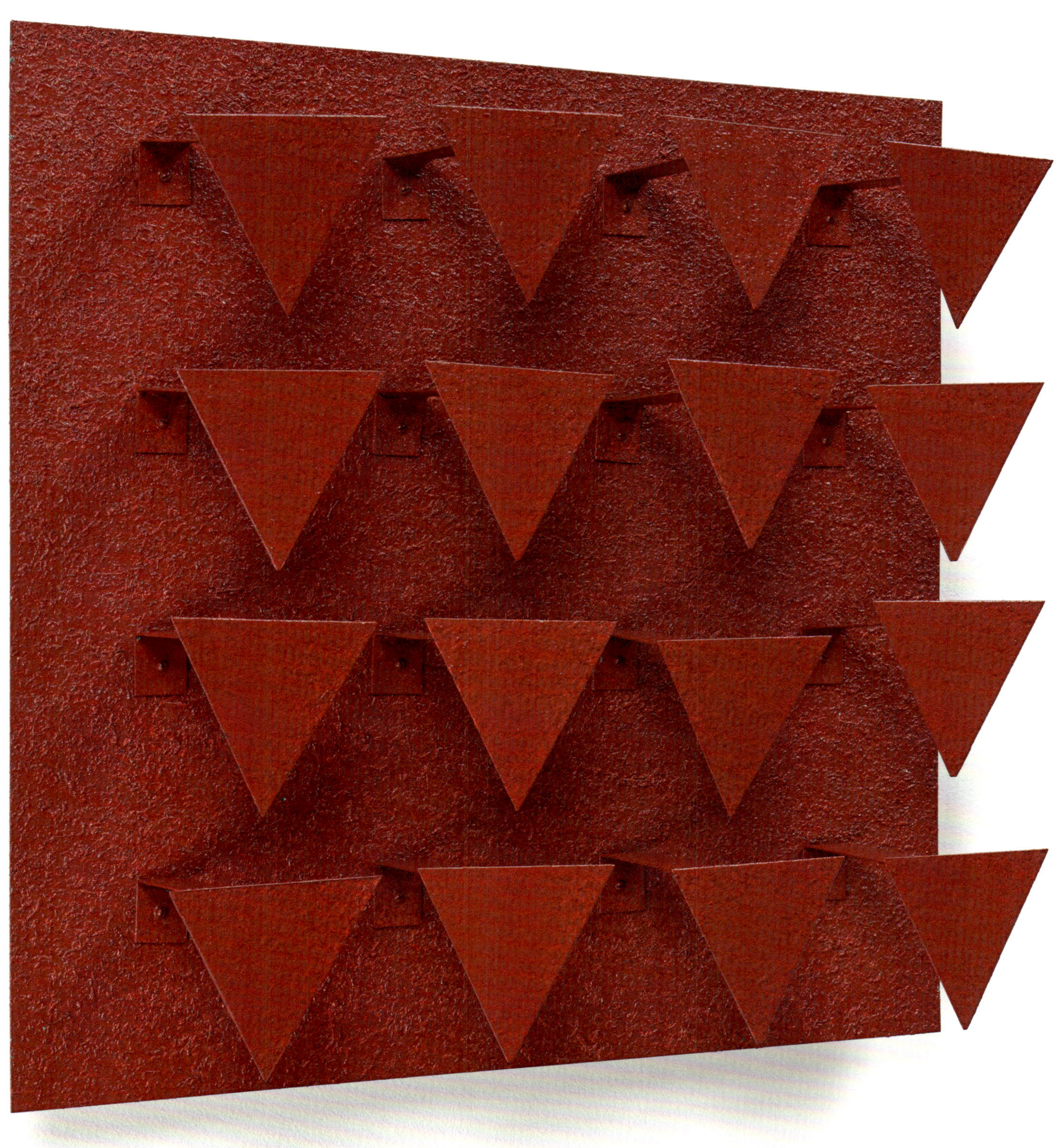

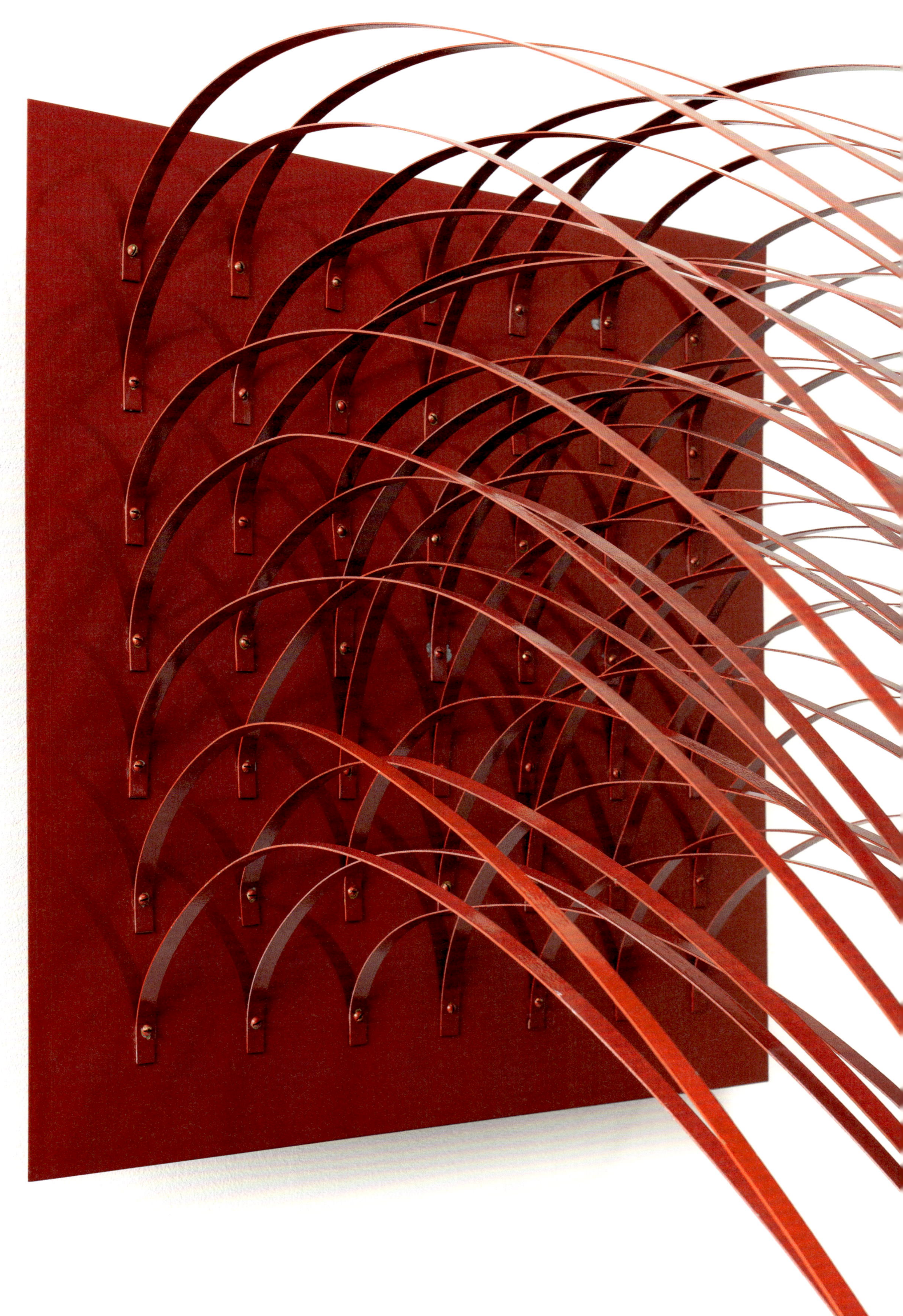

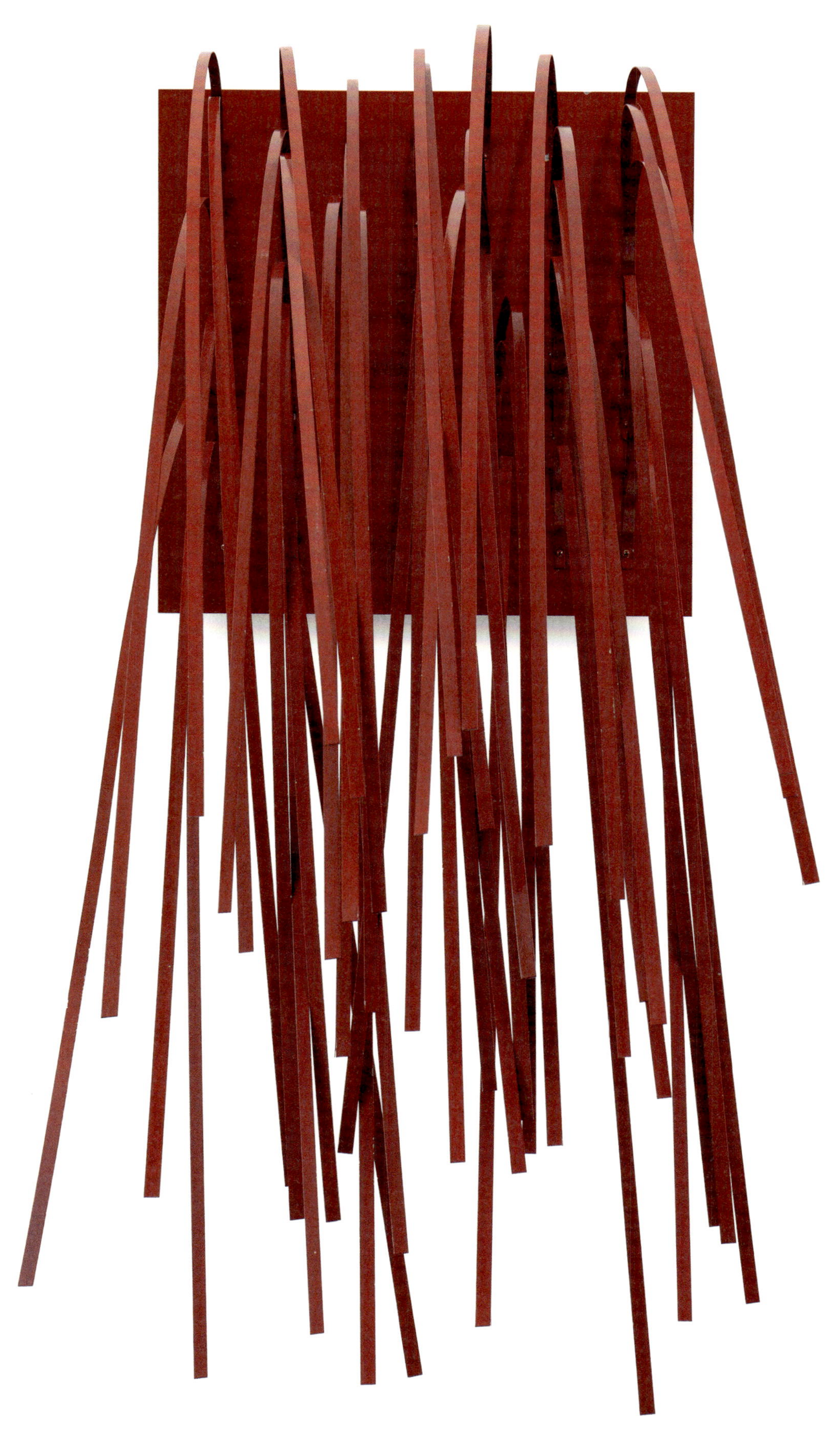

 Amazonino Vermelho (Red Amazonino), 1989/2003

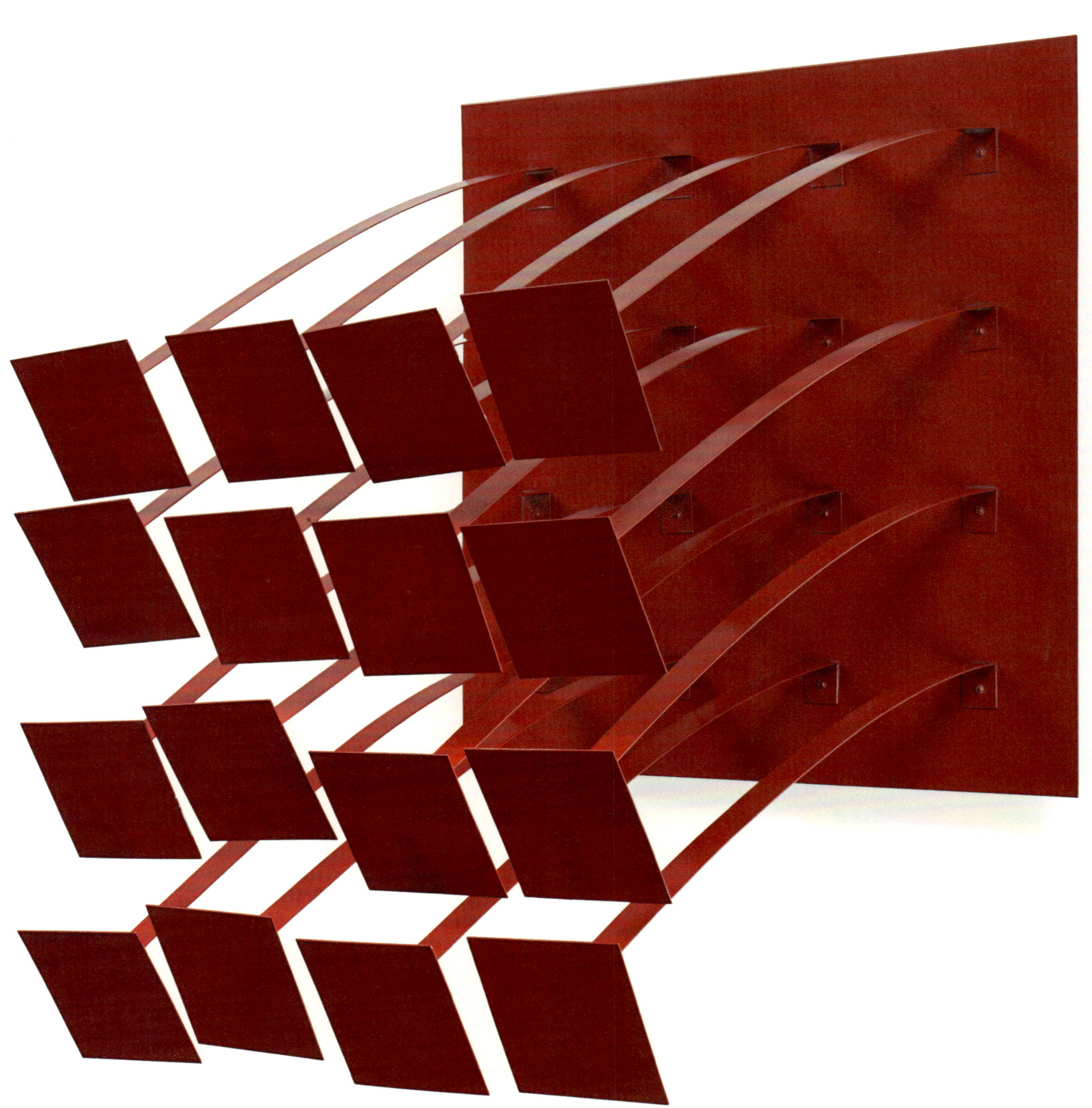

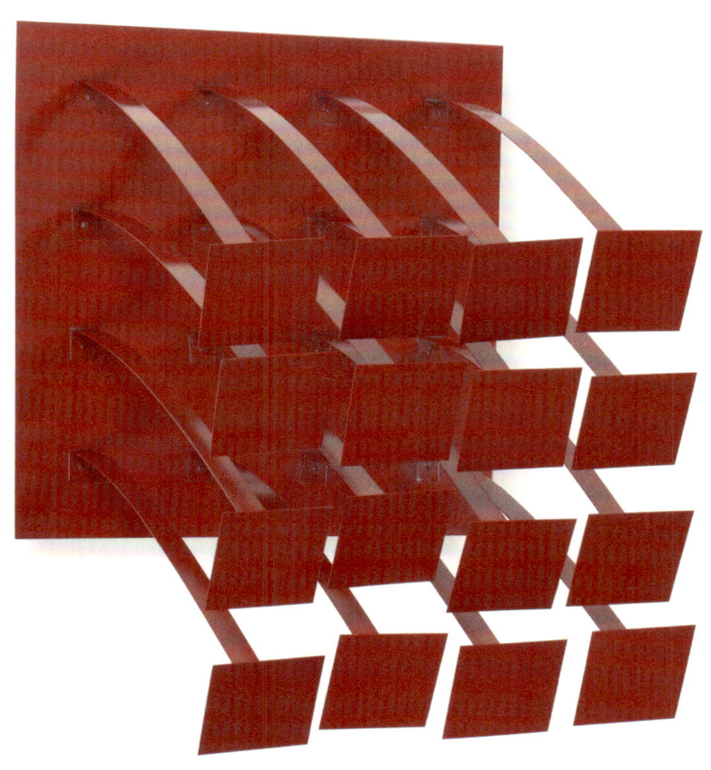

   Amazonino Vermelho (Red Amazonino), 1989/2003

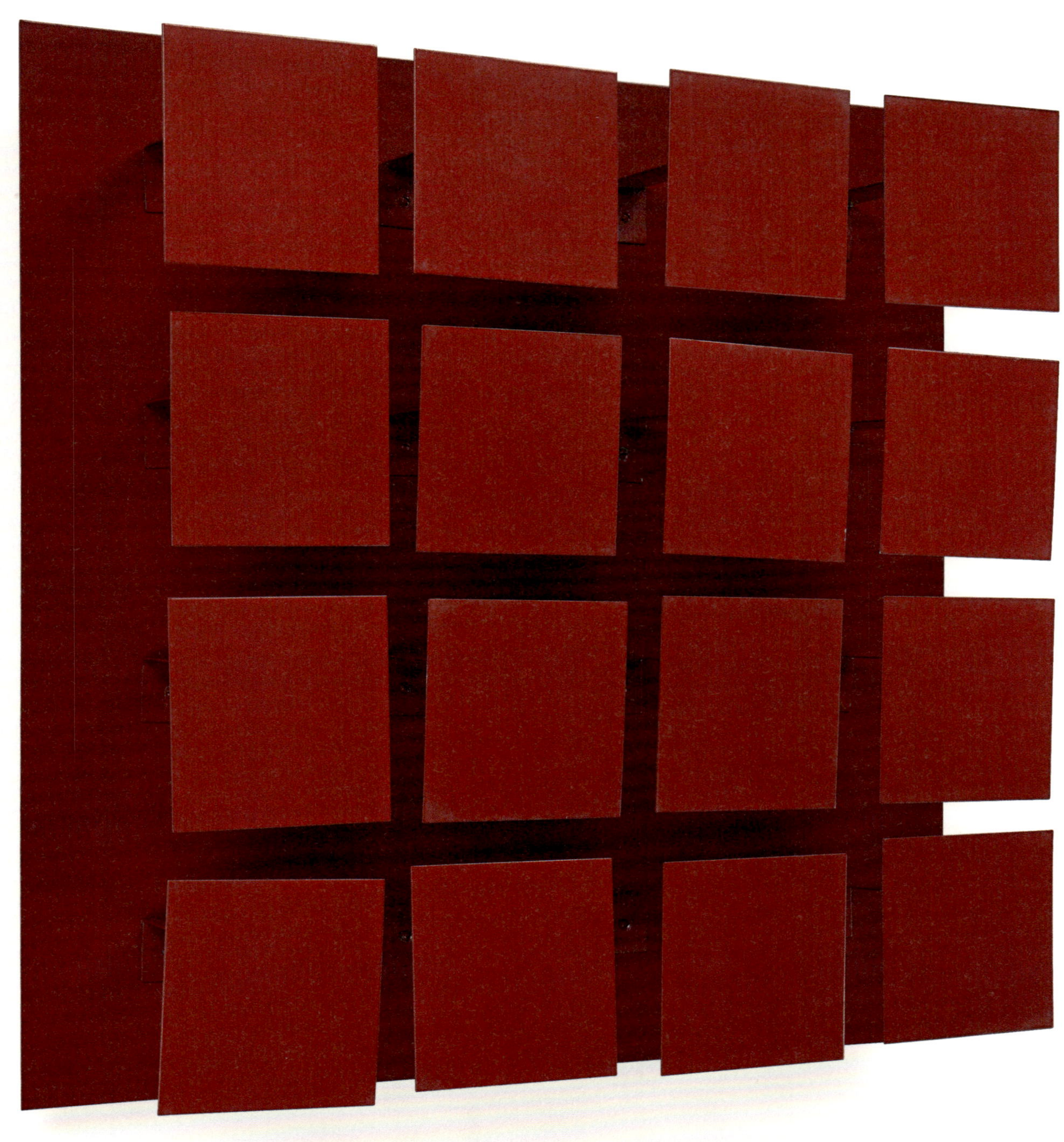

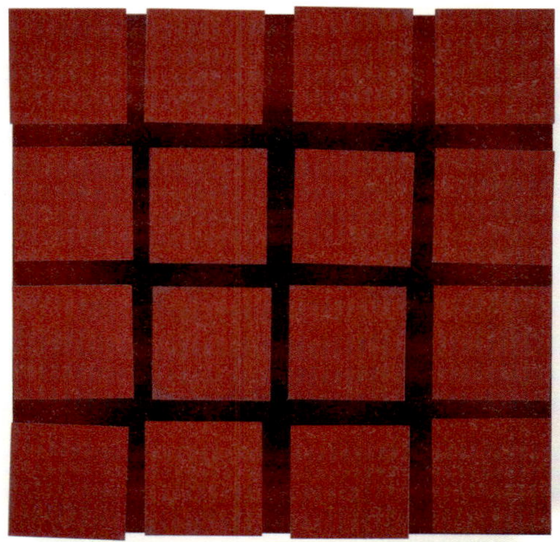

   Amazonino Vermelho (Red Amazonino), 1989/2003

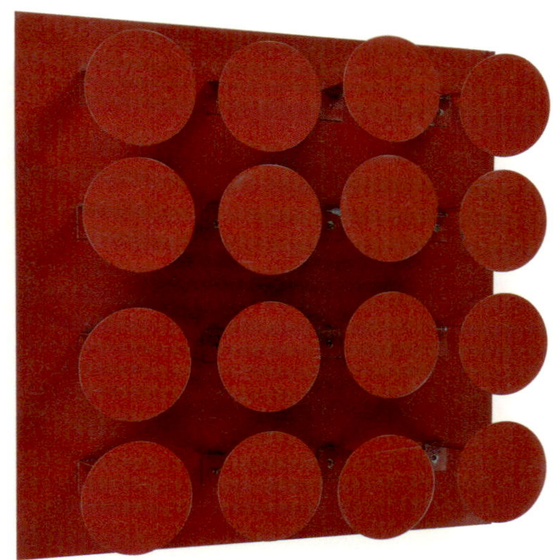

 Amazonino Vermelho (Red Amazonino), 1989/2003

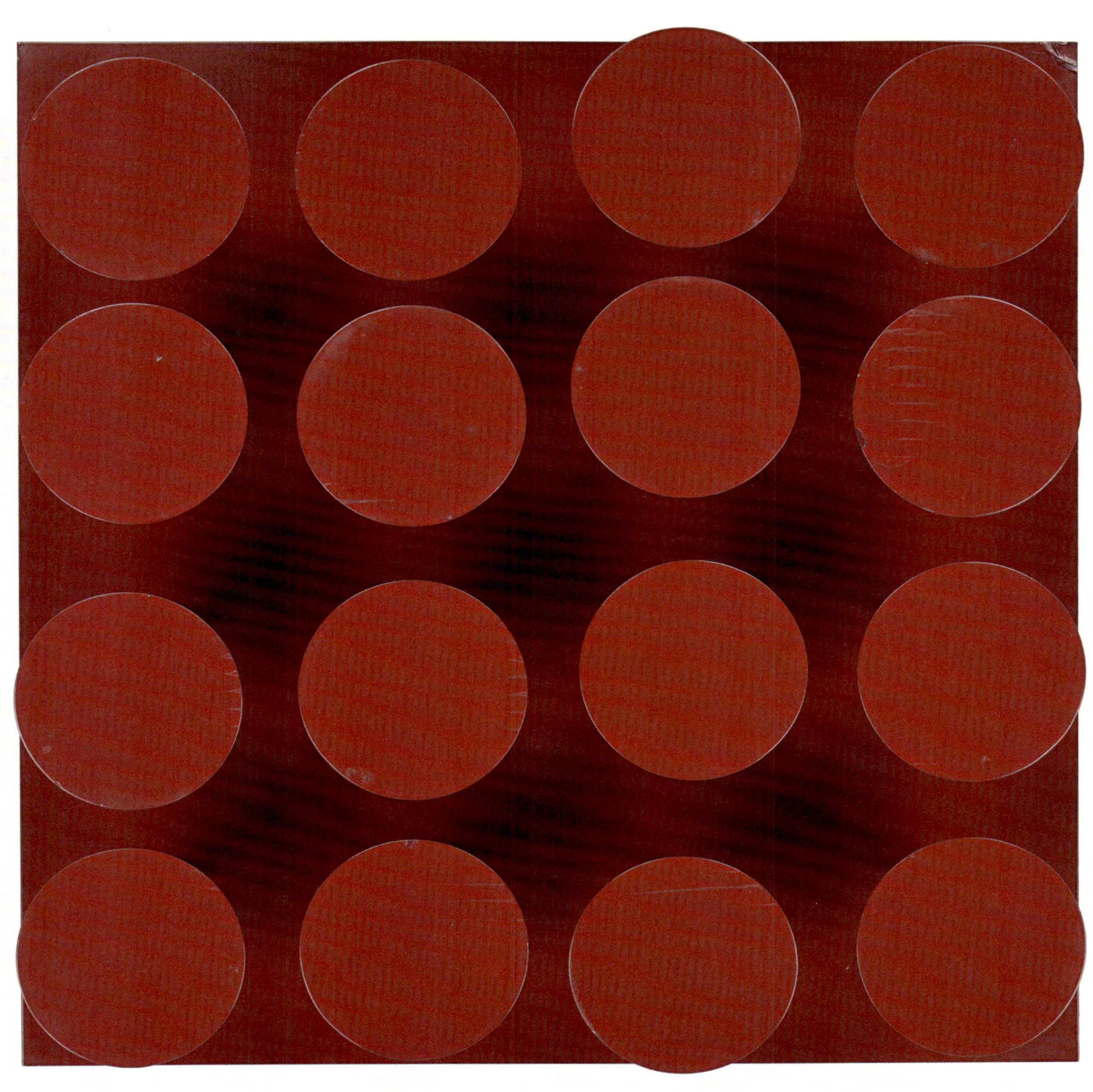

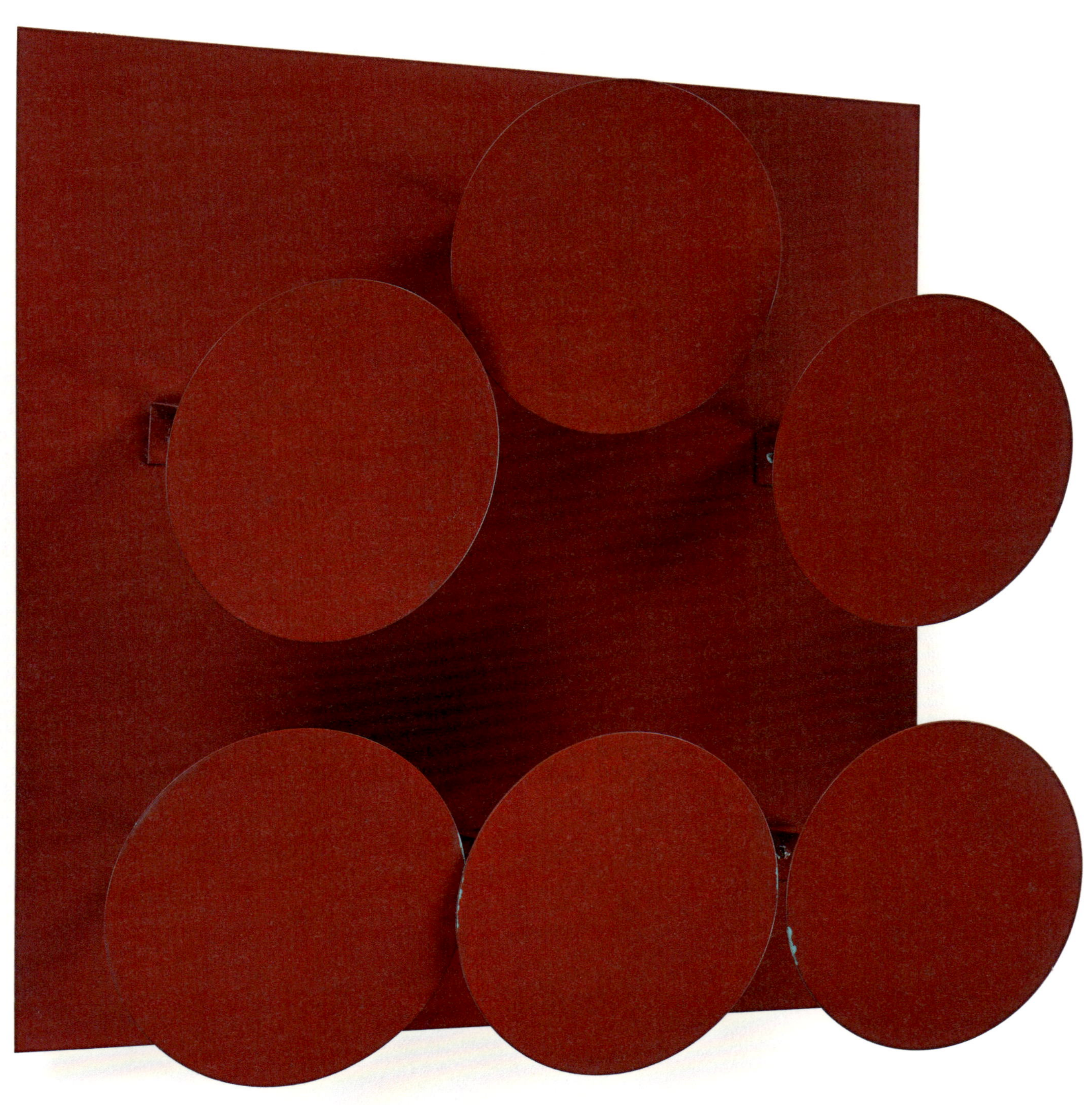

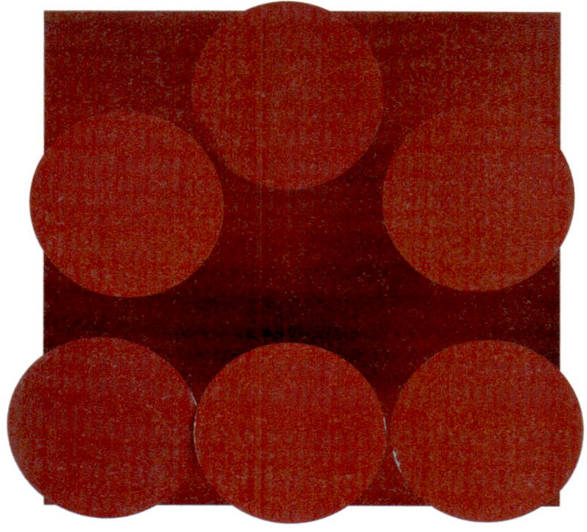

  Amazonino Vermelho (Red Amazonino), 1989/2003

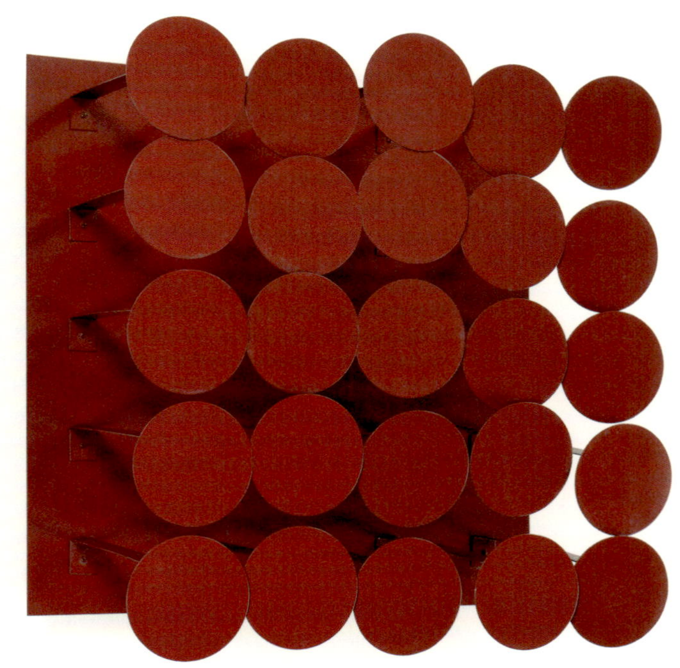

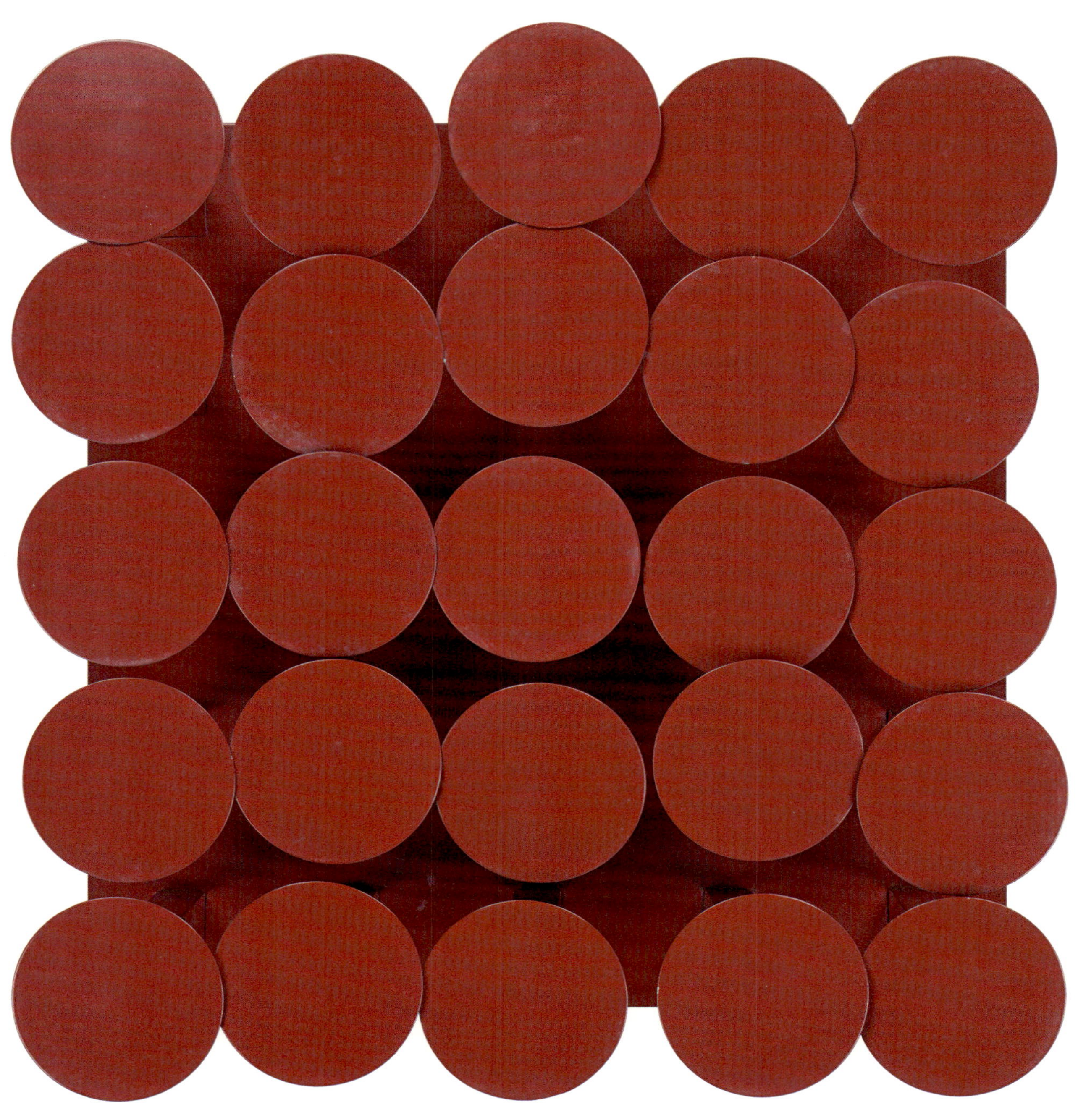

Amazonino Vermelho (Red Amazonino), 1989/2003

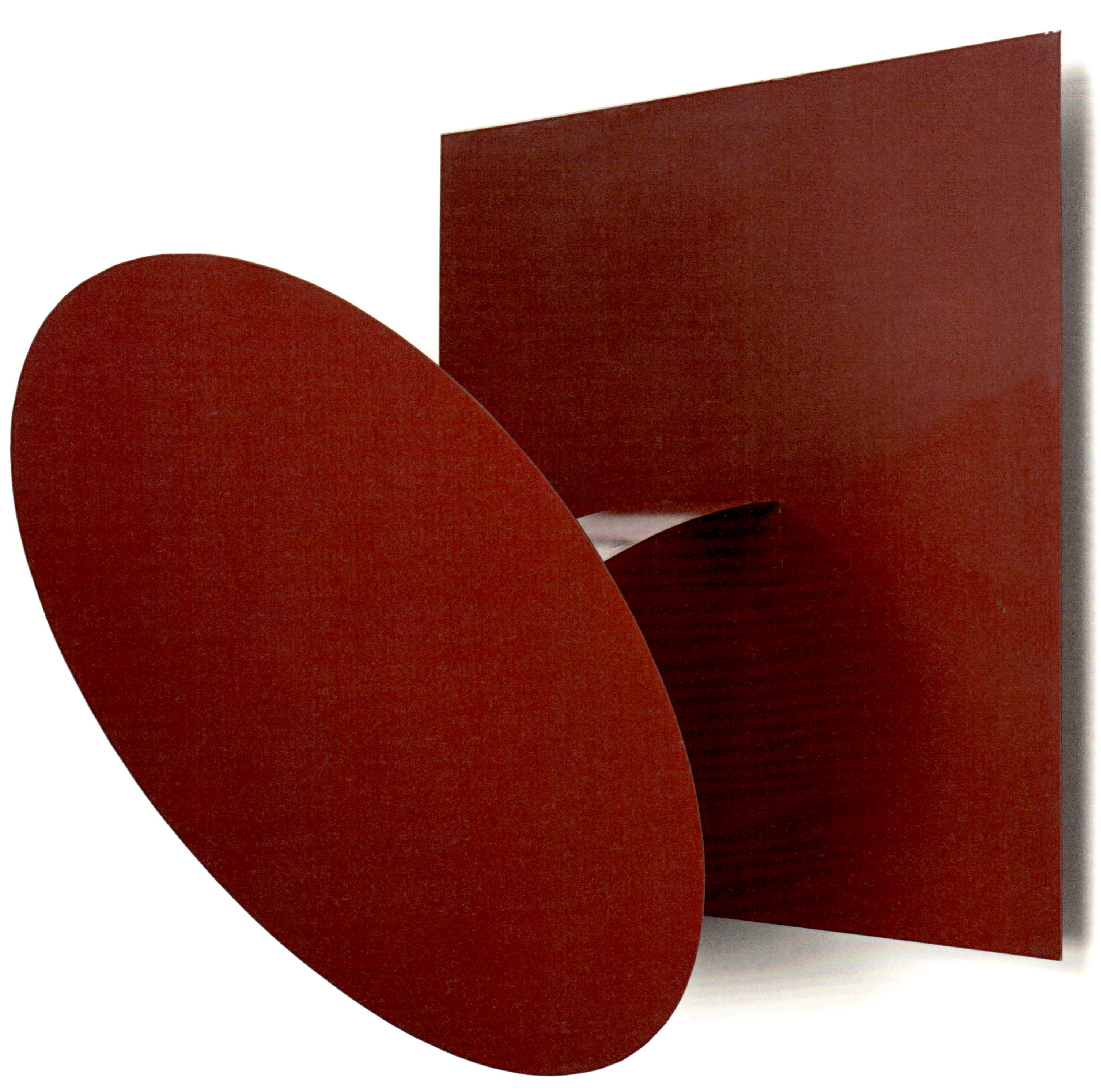

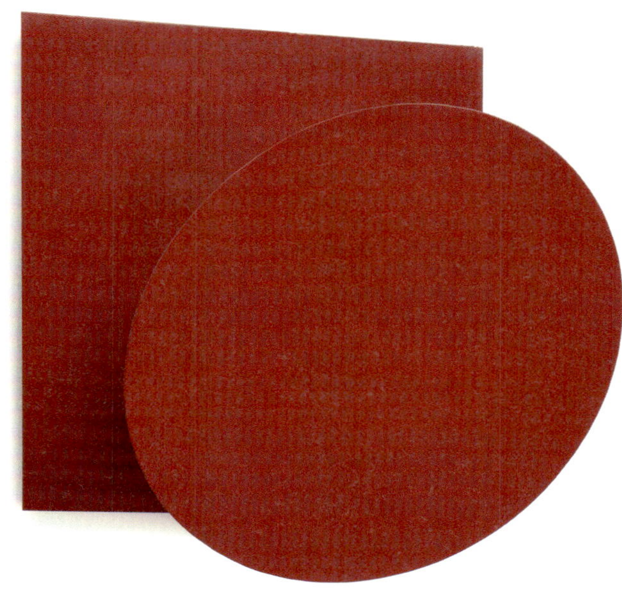

  Amazonino Vermelho (Red Amazonino), 1989/2003

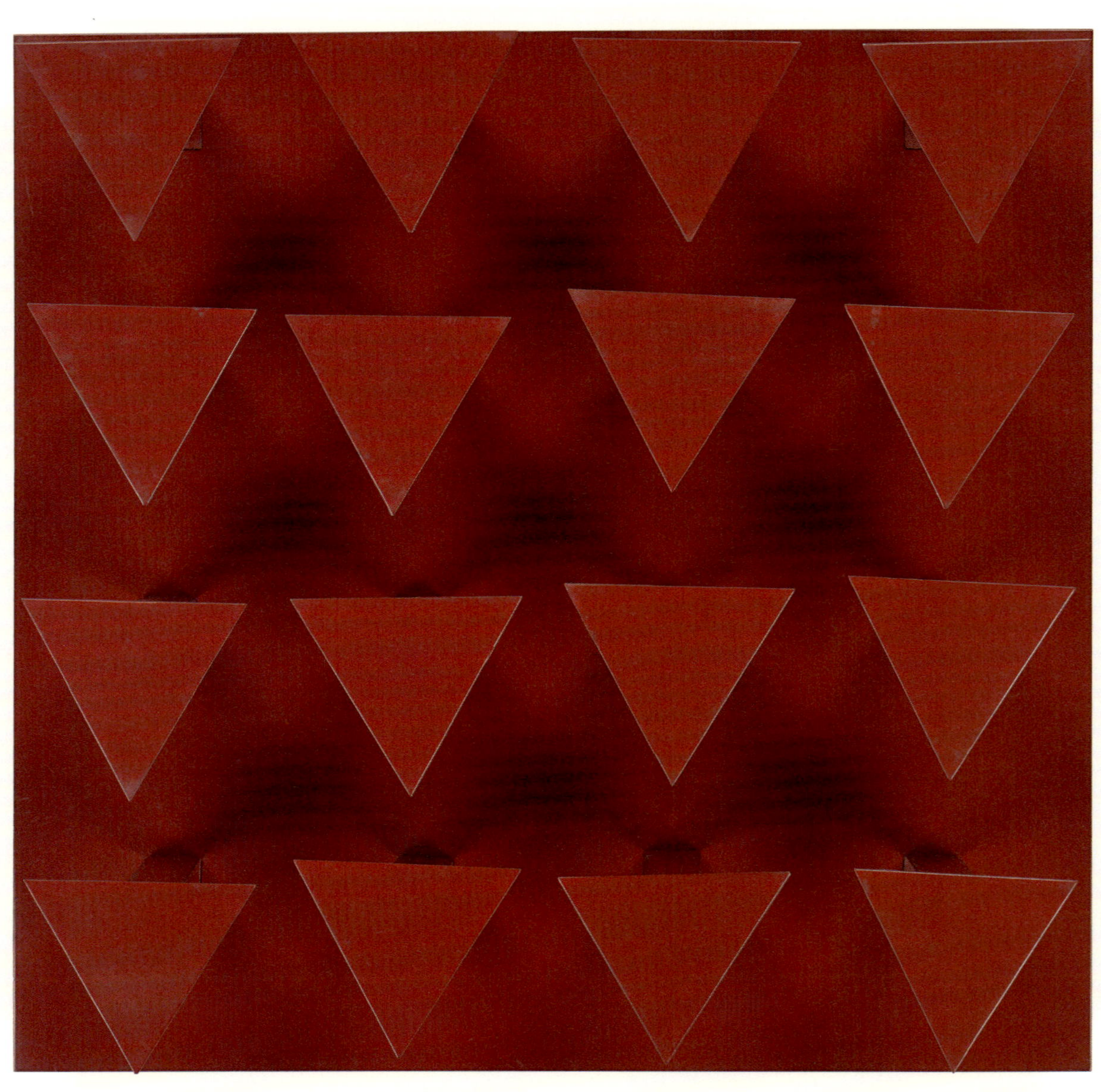

Amazonino Vermelho (Red Amazonino), 1989/2003

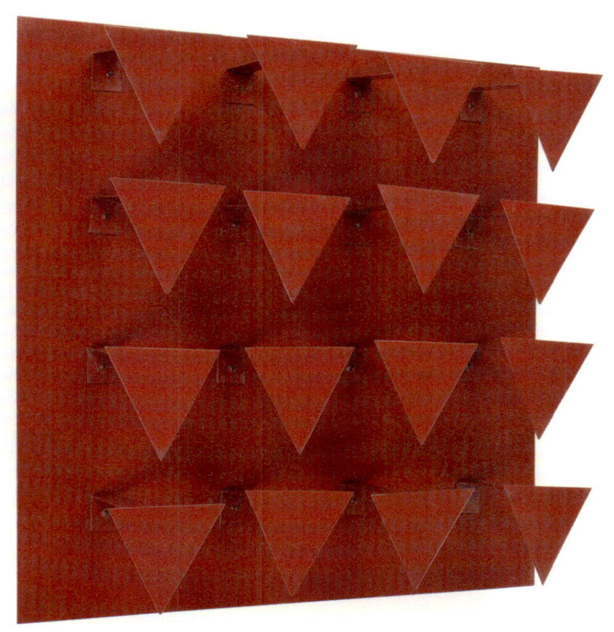

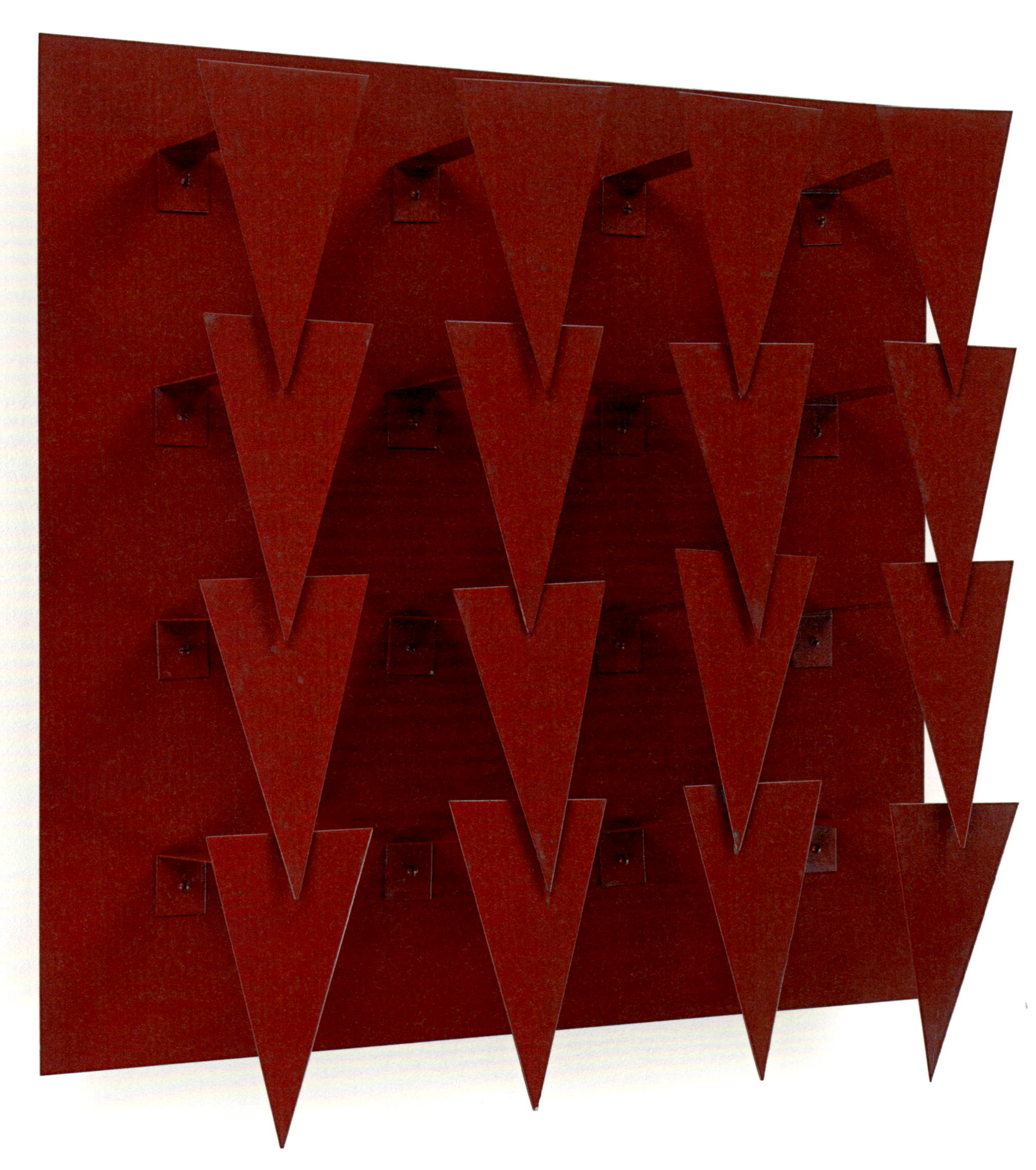

Amazonino Vermelho (Red Amazonino), 1989/2003

Paulo Herkenhoff and
Paula Pape in conversation
with Ferreira Gullar

at the home of Ferreira Gullar,
Copacabana, Rio de Janeiro,
Brazil, July 7, 2009[1]

PAULO HERKENHOFF
When did you come from Maranhão, when was it?

FERREIRA GULLAR
August '51. That was when I went to Mário [Pedrosa]'s home. When I arrived at Mario's, Lucy[2] . . . when I arrived, she took me—"look, I've already told Mário . . . that you arrived. Tomorrow we're going to his place." I realized that he was a friendly person and became his friend . . . someone intelligent, elegant and understanding, able to give me some attention at that time. I was a kid.

It was at his place that I met all these people: Lygia Pape, Lygia Clark, Amilcar [de Castro], [Franz] Weissmann, Ivan [Serpa].

When concretism arrives in Brazil, I mean concrete art . . . concrete art is an extreme expression of this process that starts in cubism: Mondrian giving a direction that is substantial, already structured, which cubism didn't have. Then it develops with [Theo van] Doesburg and, then, with the Ulm School. You see, already with Max Bill painting had become something that is basically the exploration of the dynamics of the visual field. It doesn't express anything else, doesn't want to *represent* anything, not even Malevich's metaphysics. It's like this: "I am going to explore the energies of the visual field . . ." It's almost a scientific thing, something extreme that eliminates all subjectivity. So, these folks, our concretists, inherited this, and what happened was this: it was a purely optical thing . . . and how it was transformed here in Brazil, how it was adapted . . . I think that the reaction of Rio's group, from which neoconcrete art will emerge, was the search for an alternative to a language that became so deprived of any subjectivity that it became a retinal, optical phenomenon. And that will culminate in something that is the opposite, which is the corporeal and the tactile. In fact, neoconcretism was called *anti*-concretism, because it dissolved and destroyed that; it became its opposite.

PH
Take Lygia Pape, for instance. I think she has a trajectory that reaches the organic by firstly going through the question of figuration, but with organic forms from the outset . . . a kind of sinuous, amoeboid line.

From there, she understands—in her woodcuts—the question of organicity, and moves on to a different level, to another moment that would be the very *language* of woodcut engraving. In this process, the question of rupture, the differences [that emerged] . . . I wanted to follow what you said, but also take in some facts: the *National Exhibition of Concrete Art* was, in fact, a milestone, because it gathered a number of artists—not all, but a very significant number—around that question, [those who were] showing a certain rigor, a certain "knowing" [*sabença*], as Mário Pedrosa would say, versus the intuition of Rio de Janeiro.[3] He wrote the article "Paulistas and Cariocas"[4] in which he highlights these differences, and I read this article today, from a distance, almost as a "slap on the wrist" for Rio's group, because his theoretical work had gained such intensity, such presence, dynamism.

Lygia Clark began to write, Hélio [Oiticica], Lygia Pape. . . . It served to say, look, we need a different kind of attitude regarding reflection. So, what was produced after [Mário's] article of 1957 . . . the exhibition was in 1956, in 1957 he comes to Rio and writes the article, in February '57 . . . what is written between February '57 and 1960/61 is extraordinary.

FG

I remember that Mário called me to his place [*laughs*] and . . . that "slap on the wrist" was very delicate, he hinted that . . . I remember well, he said: "I understand their position, but one must take into account that they had something important, which is the consciousness that they were making History—and this cannot be underestimated. I understand your disquietude, the disagreement and all." It turns out that the disagreement came precisely from that perception, because my roots are not concretist, it has nothing [to do with it] and, on the contrary, [that interpretation] is at the limit of irrationality. *A luta corporal* [The body's struggle] is a book that ends with the inclusion of language. It's the attempt to overcome the relation Order/Disorder, to create something else.[5]

But I went home and wrote "Theory of the Non-object."[6] It had to do with what everybody was doing, with what Amilcar was doing, with what Lygia Pape was doing, what Hélio was doing. It had to do with it because it

wasn't any more like "I am making a painting; I am making a print; I am making a sculpture"—it wasn't! Even a sculpture by Amilcar was no longer . . . it was a plaque, he cut it and pulled one part. . . . So, what *was* that?

PAULA PAPE

They were manifestations!

FG

Yes, that was a process common to all [of them].

PH

Ferreira Gullar, I think that it was as much an *object*, what Lygia [Clark] was making, but also what Lygia Pape, Amilcar, and Hélio were producing. In their reaction, there's information behind it that allows us to reach that conclusion, those visual and theoretical conclusions.

In fact, you had already been very clear with Pedrosa, with the artists, about certain parameters of Western History that brought about a position from which the Artist had necessarily to respond, still within an art system and a fairly narrow historical process. I think Mondrian and Malevich set out this point, and the understanding of history of art, that I see with Mário Pedrosa, with you, and also in these artists' practices: that the history of art is not a sequence of "isms" to be followed (which would be a marketing thing). It's not a group of heroes of form, as Malevich said. Also, it isn't a question of images to be interpreted; maybe there are irresolute problems of form. That is, the Mondrian that would be of interest is the one that Mondrian himself was unable to produce. It's that crossing of a limit, almost as if authorship was dissolved and problems were floating.

[However,] I think that this is not important, neither that there was an awareness of it, except at that moment one discusses the question of the artistic object with such clarity. You go through a process of elimination. Also, we shouldn't forget that, through different paths, Mondrian and Malevich thought that the way these formal explorations unfolded would necessarily lead to the dissolution of the object. Isn't that so? It's that limit, which is not the end of painting—one shouldn't mix it with the pedestrian question of the end of painting.

It was much more the understanding that there would be a logic of form.

So I find that when there's that encounter between artists and theorists . . . in fact, I find it a giant step taken by Brazilian art of all times, facing the History of Western Art.

What I think will be [seen as] a major drive of Rio de Janeiro's art is the presence of the two critics [Pedrosa and Gullar] alongside such a productive generation. That imbrication between theory [and art], that opening through theory, that search to understand "cuts" [*cortes*] in language . . . I think it was crucial, as if the artists taught the critics to consider the new art, while the critics clarified that discourse. You are one of those who fully fits into this sense of the term—

FG

Just, I didn't know—

PH

No, I think you knew—

FG

I was saying, I didn't know that concrete art was the end of something, that's a tendency [of the discourse] that I don't agree with . . .

PH

[But] it reaches an impasse that for you had already been announced in Maranhão, when you read Mário's thesis[7] . . . what you understand from Mário's thesis (which is from previous years), which might represent the direction that he was starting to take . . . if it didn't start with you yourself. I cannot say right now. But I think that what the neoconcrete experience points out (the position that you advance here, your relation to Mário's thesis, etc.) is an understanding of the gestalt question with its rules. In a certain sense it was a prescription for an art of the predictable, and Theo van Doesburg says that neoconcrete art has that predictability.

It is, therefore, a type of art that is supported by the mechanical functioning of the brain, mental laws; whereas phenomenology opens up a different relationship with the subject. It is the vision of Merleau-Ponty's phenomenology, because [neoconcretism] happens in parallel to what's happening in France, simultaneously, and before what is going to happen in the United States during the 1960s. The Brazilians read Merleau-Ponty before a certain American group. How was it for you, that encounter with Merleau-Ponty's phenomenology?

FG

[It came about] through discussing these issues at Mário's place. I would put forward some issues and Mário would say "these comments that you are saying . . . maybe you should read Merleau-Ponty." . . . "I want to read," [I replied]. "I have here a book that I can lend to you: it's *La structure du comportement* [The Structure of Behavior]."[8] He then lent me the book and I took it home and, as I read it, I realized that it answered the questions that I was posing and for which I had no answer. So, when I read Merleau-Ponty, I saw a different perspective . . . there is a truth that is of science, but there is a truth that is of the experience of the world. And Lygia [Pape] made the *Book of Creation*.[9]

What is interesting about the group is that everyone exchanged experiences.

PH

We have an "Albersian" model [Josef Albers] that was important, we have the homage to the square, a proliferating homage to the square . . .

FG

That comes from Malevich—

PH

That comes from Malevich but also passes through Albers—

FG

Yes because he also makes [squares], but he makes them in different colors and overlapping [each other].

PH

So we have the *Book of Creation*. In fact, these are pages that pay tribute to the square. It can be read like that.

FG

Discovering Albers was quite enriching, do you understand? When we discovered Albers—

PH

What does it mean, "to discover"? Seeing an exhibition? Reading books, magazines . . . ?

FG

To see, to see things . . . today, it is much easier to have access to everything, but back then, to discover certain things . . . I only discovered Tatlin's works and other things because I shopped by chance in the French bookshop in [Avenida Presidente] Antônio Carlos. So I got a book by Michel Seuphor, which is *L'art abstrait* [Abstract art].[10] At that time, this book was the only one with reproductions of unknown works by Malevich, Tatlin, and Rodchenko.

PP

Now, I think . . . that group—Pape, Clark, Oiticica—I experienced all that as well. I was an eyewitness because I would go the Modern Art Museum [of Rio de Janeiro] and socialize at Hélio's place. I would mingle with them. That was the dynamic: this thing about the new; non-repetition; creation, pure creation . . .

FG

To construct something . . .

PP

To construct something. . . . Now, what I also see in Lygia, something that strikes me in her work is that, from the '50s, she was also a poet. Do you understand? She was a poet, searching in forms as well as in words. What do you feel when, for instance, you see the word in the work [of art]?

FG

That conjunction of the word with the constructed form is something born of neoconcrete art, because before, it didn't exist—do you understand? So, the different members of the group . . . because for the first time it connected the poet and the painter, you see? So, the word comes from the poets, from [Theon] Spanudius, Reynaldo Jardim, and my works. That junction of poets and painters was very productive and not only the poets started applying color in their work and visual [plastic] elements . . .

PP

Yes, there was a healthy exchange . . .

FG

I think that is one of the elements, one of the innovations that arises with the neoconcrete movement, that is present in Lygia Pape's work.

PP

Yes, there was the *Book of Creation* where, in fact, she does not use words . . . everyone [each viewer] is going to create the word. . . . But in certain moments she uses words.

FG

There was this junction of the visual [plastic] thing with the word, but Amilcar doesn't have it, Weissmann doesn't have it, [Aluísio] Carvão doesn't have it, Lygia Clark doesn't have it. . . . Lygia Pape is from fine arts, she is the only one who connects both things, like the poets did, but in reverse, starting from the word using visual [plastic] forms. But I think this is an innovation of the neoconcrete movement.

In Lygia Pape's case, it is something more open, she uncovers unexpected things; perhaps . . . even because of the poetic character of that connection with the word, of making the *Book of Creation*, which are almost symbolic forms. It isn't a direct material thing as it was with Hélio.

PP

You met Lygia right at the beginning, right? And you realized that she was an artist who would produce continuously until the end of her days.

FG

It was her vocation, her necessity. Those who are not like that remain half of the way. In some cases, even those who are like that stay halfway, but they are rare. In most cases, it is the life of the person, like Lygia Pape, who committed the whole of her life [to creating art]. There's nothing stopping you. You can have moments when you stop for reasons to do with your [daily] life or something else—but you come back because that is the riverbed of your work, your path, and is the thing that really matters to you, through which you invent and affirm yourself. Something quite particular, which is always the search for that "mastery" [*superação*]. Real artists are like that.

PP
You must have met me when I was very little . . .

FG
But I remember you very well . . . funny, how you look like your mum.

1. Translated from the Portuguese by Nuno Rodrigues, 2018.

2. Lucy Teixeira, a poet from Maranhão and friend of Mário Pedrosa and Ferreira Gullar.

3. *Exposição nacional de arte concreta: artes visuais poesia*, Museu de Arte Moderna São Paulo (MAM-SP), December 4–18, 1956.

4. *Paulista*: someone from São Paulo; *Carioca*: someone from Rio de Janeiro. Mário Pedrosa, "Paulistas e Cariocas," *Jornal do Brasil* (Rio de Janeiro), February 19, 1957. Translated by Stephen Berg as "Paulistas and Cariocas," in *Mário Pedrosa: Primary Documents* (New York: Museum of Modern Art, 2015), 274–75.

5. Ferreira Gullar, *A luta corporal* [The body's struggle], rev. ed. (1954; reprinted with an essay by Miguel Conde, São Paulo: Companhia das Letras, 2017).

6. Ferreira Gullar, "Teoria do não-objeto," Sunday supplement, *Jornal do Brasil* (Rio de Janeiro), December 19–20, 1959. Translated by Stephen Berg as "Theory of the Non-object," in *Mário Pedrosa: Primary Documents* (New York: Museum of Modern Art, 2015).

7. Mário Pedrosa, "Da natureza afetiva da forma na obra de arte" [On the affective nature of form in the work of art] (PhD diss., School of Architecture, Rio de Janeiro, 1949).

8. Maurice Merleau-Ponty, *La structure du comportement* (Paris: Presses universitaires de France, 1949). Translated by Alden L. Fisher as *The Structure of Behavior* (Boston: Beacon Press, 1963).

9. Lygia Pape, *Livro da Criação* (Book of Creation), 1959–60. Gouache on cardboard, 16 pieces, variable dimensions. The reader constructs a narrative from his or her interpretation of individual abstract, geometric compositions that describe the creation of the world.

10. Michel Seuphor [Fernand-Louis Berckelaers], *L'art abstrait: Ses origines, ses premiers maîtres* [Abstract art: Its origins, its first masters] (Paris: Maeght, 1949).

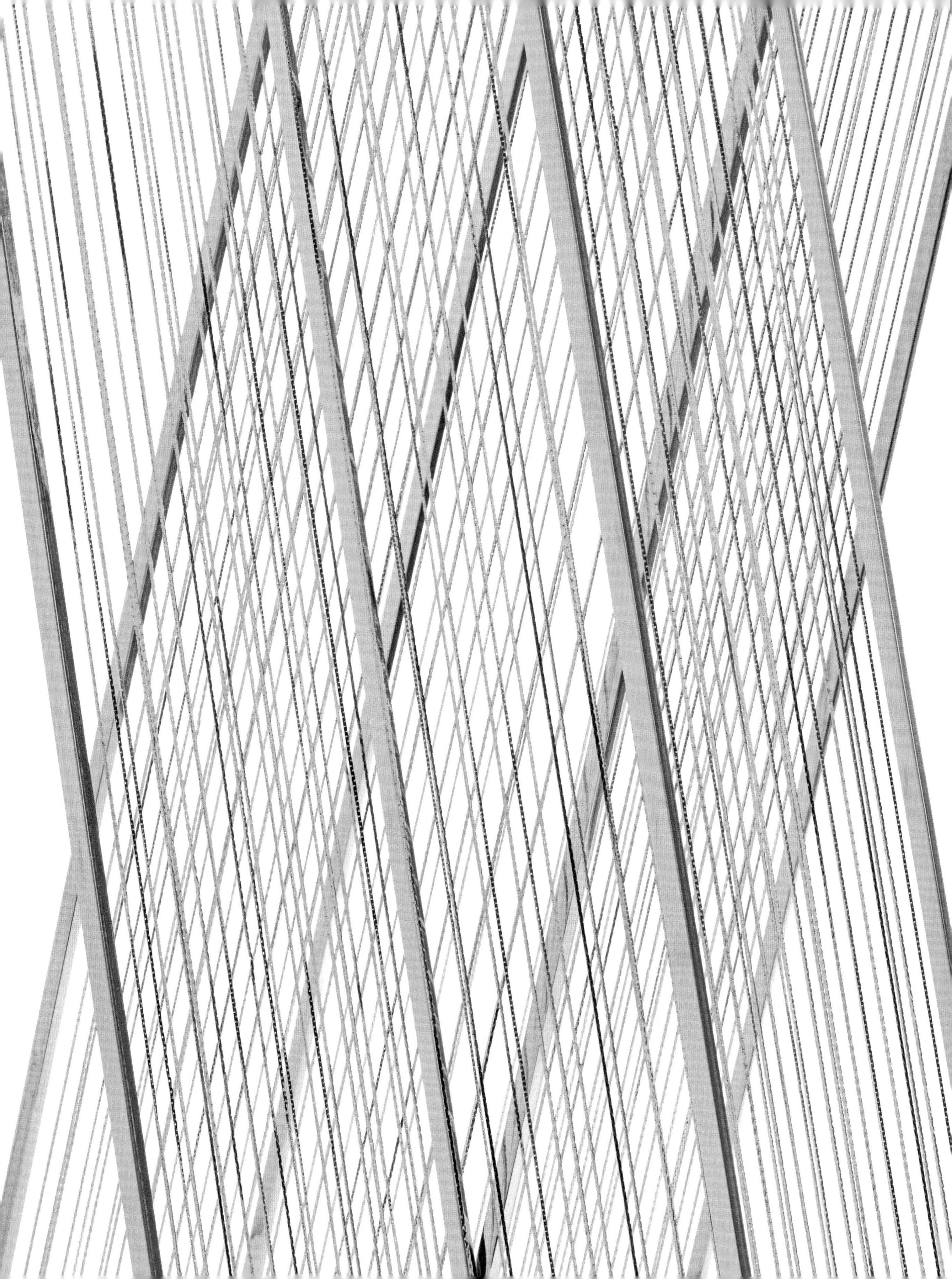

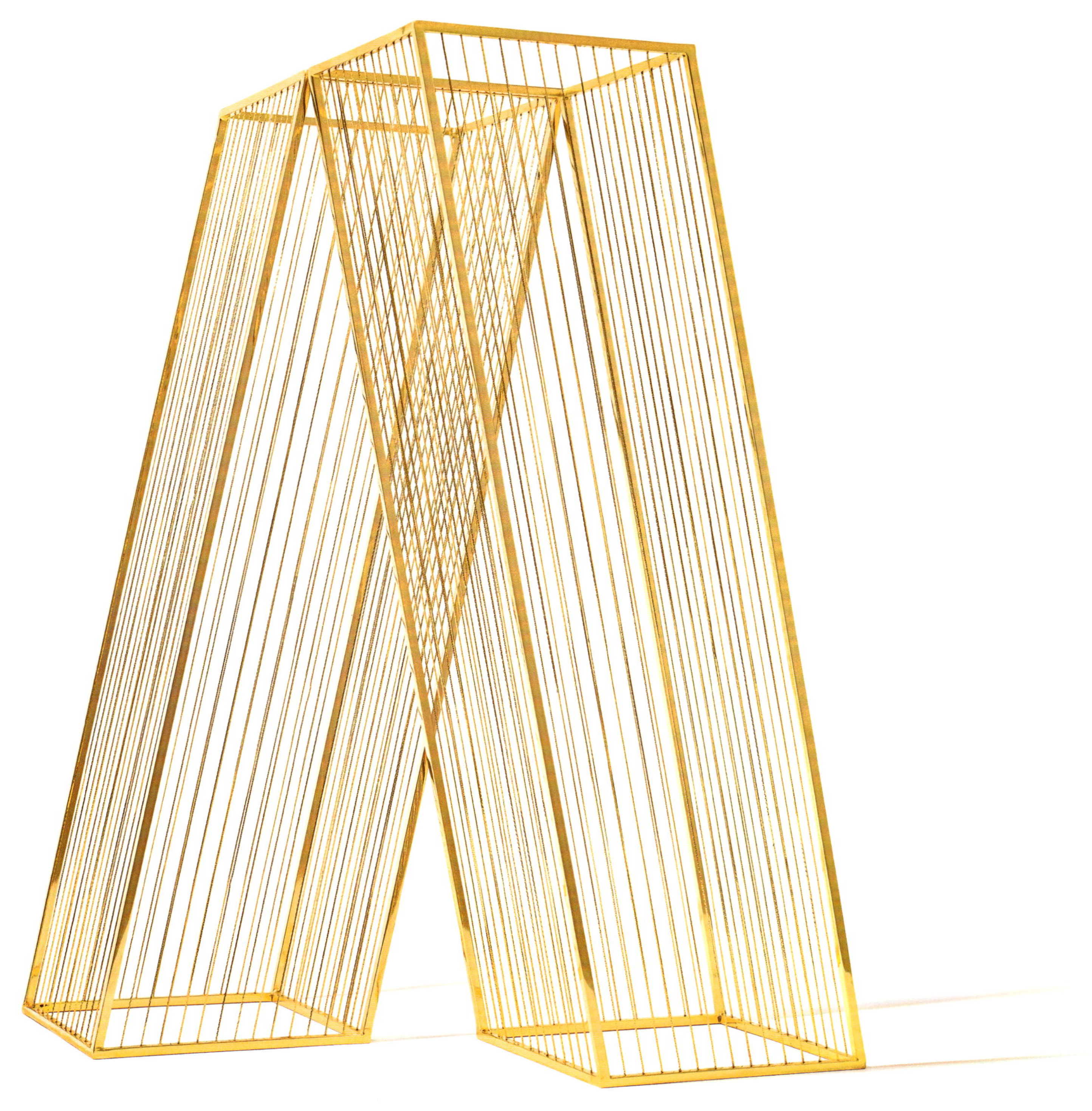

Ttéia 1, C, Metallic #1, 2003

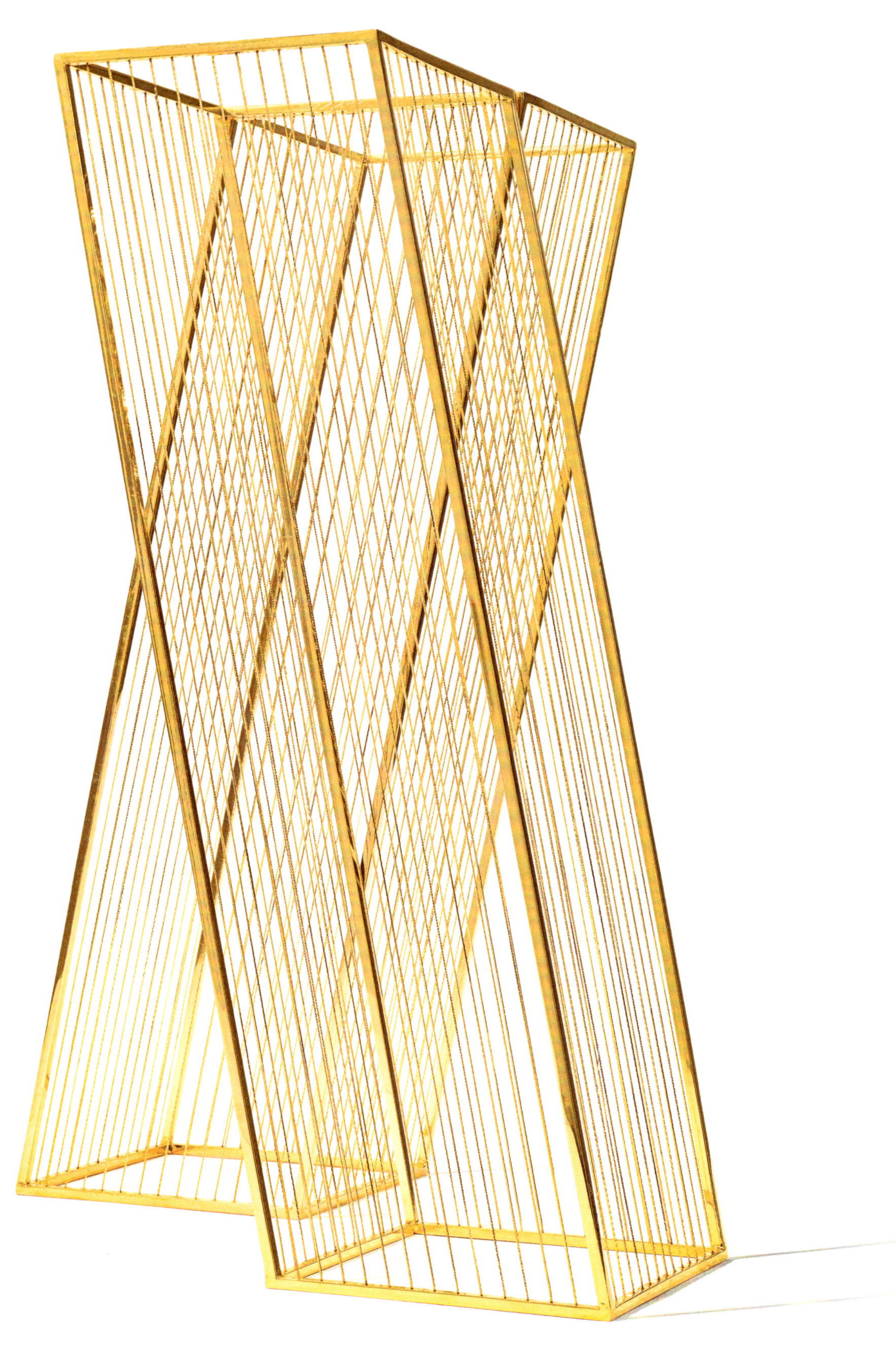

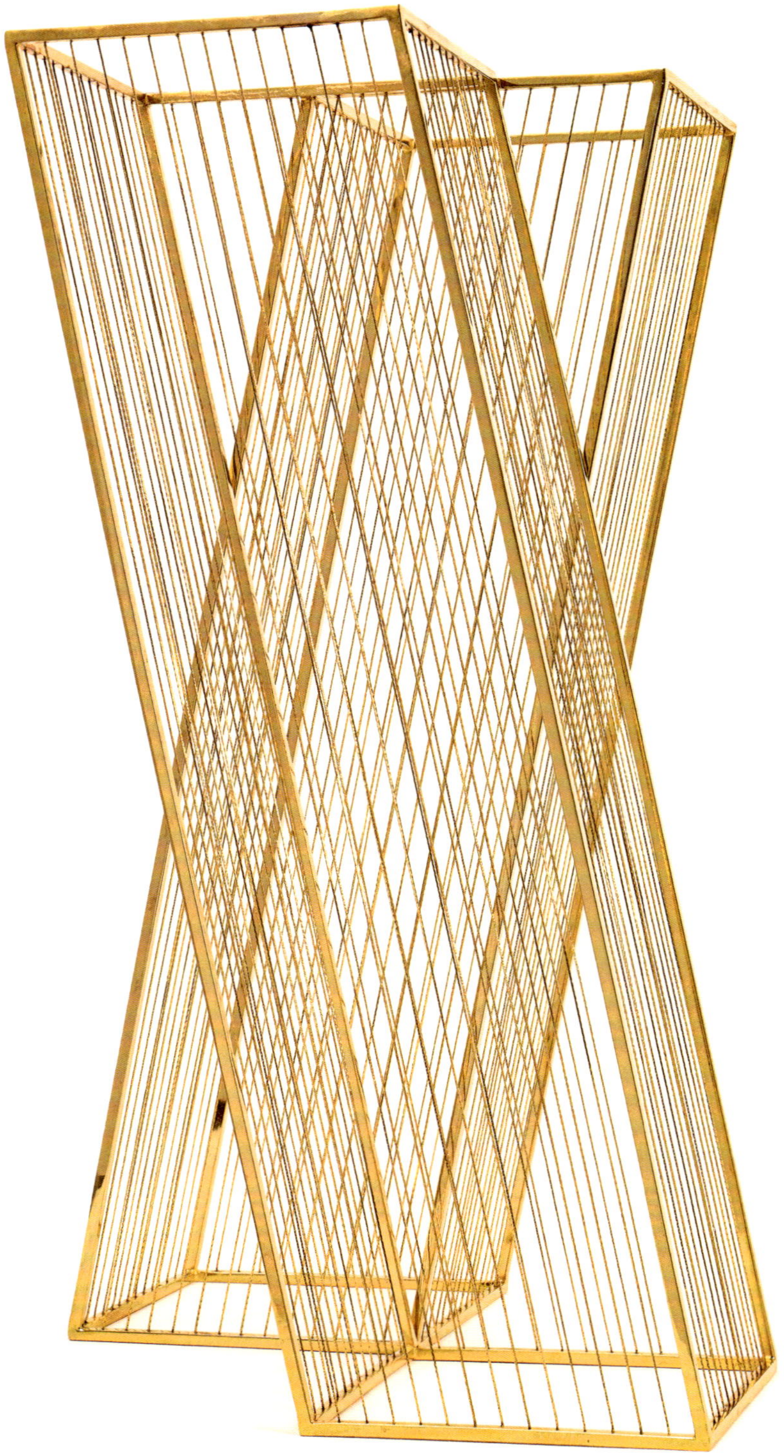

Ttéia 1, C, Metallic #2, 2003

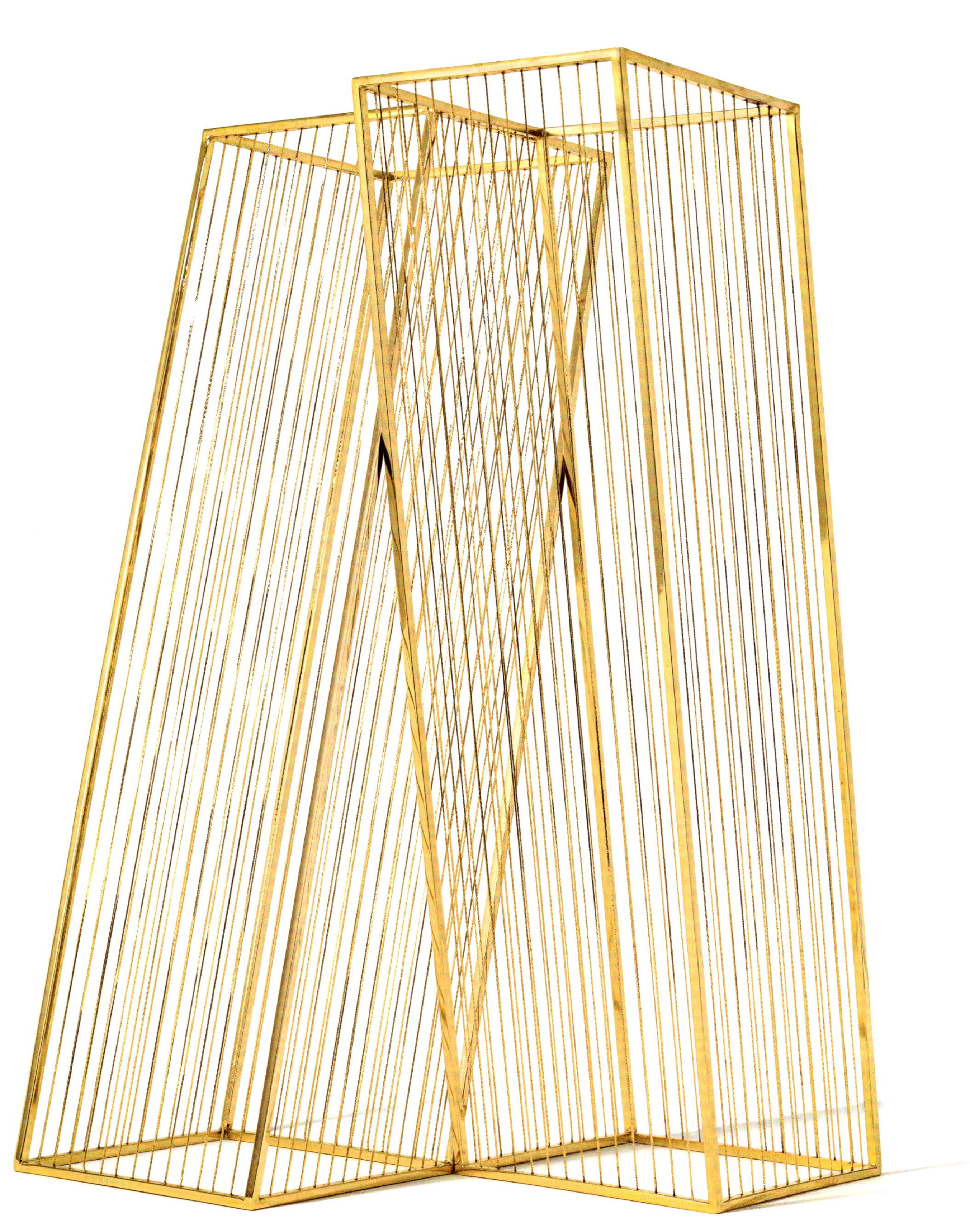

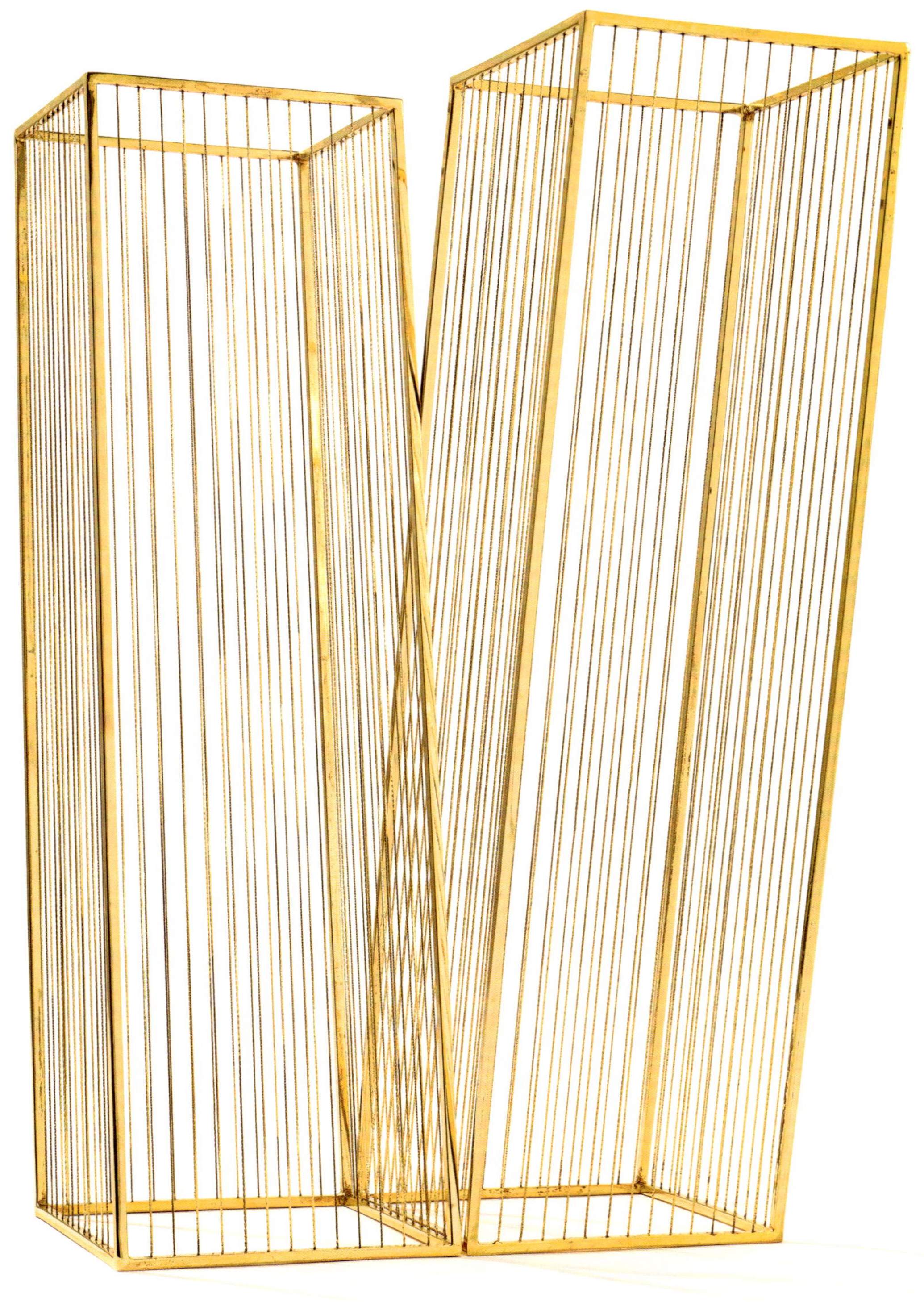

Ttéia 1, C, Metallic #3, 2003

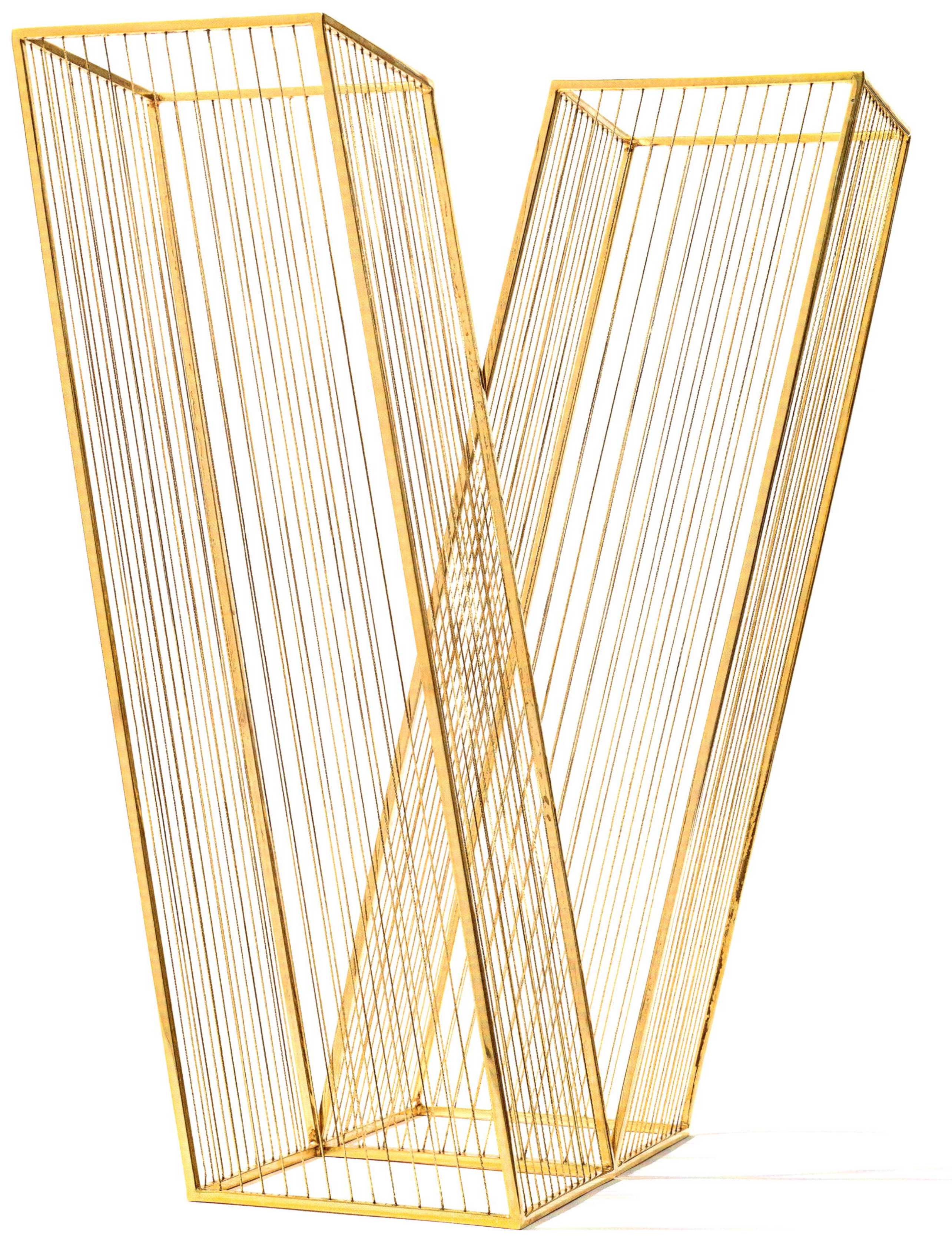

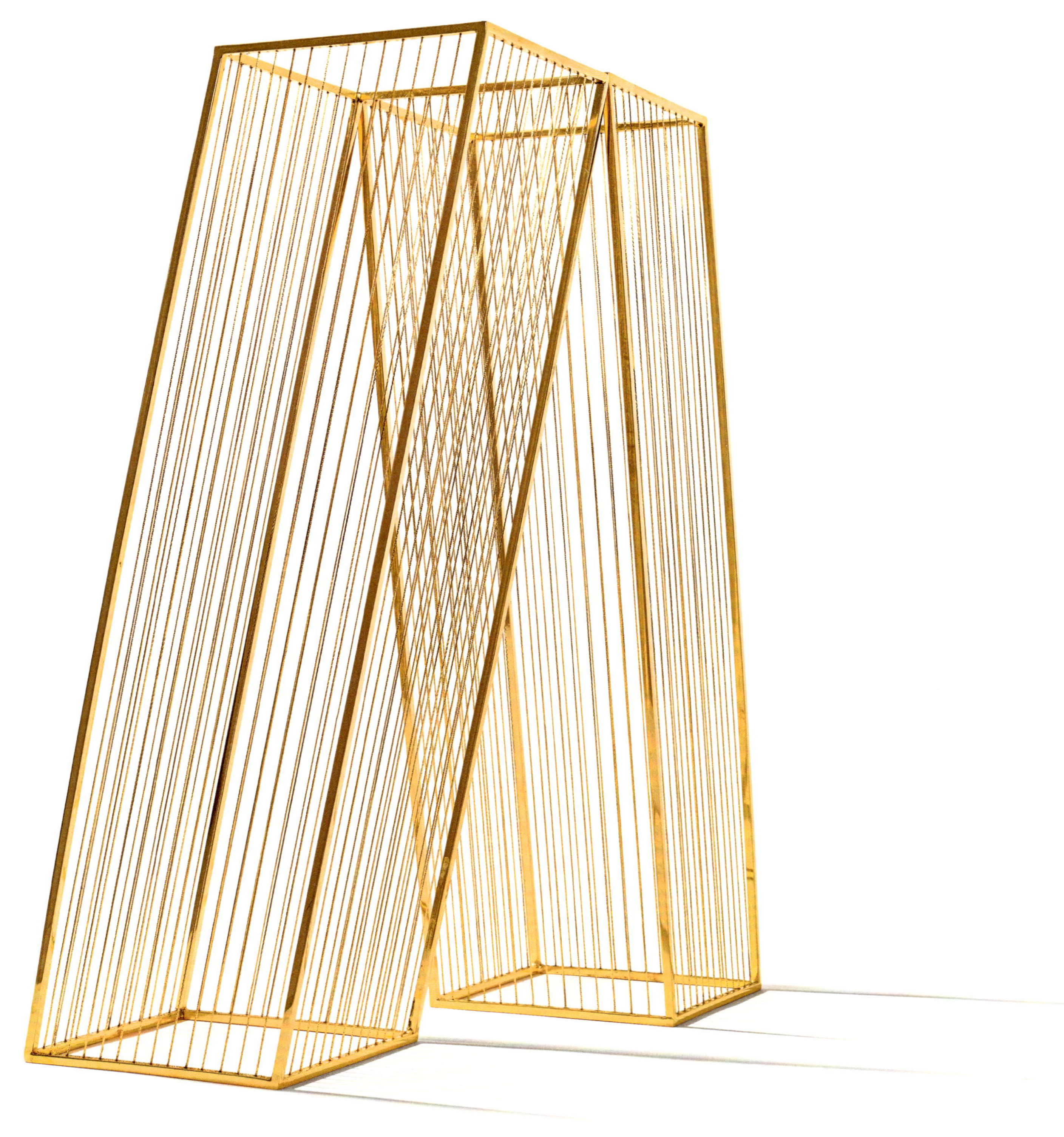

Ttéia 1, C, Metallic #4, 2003

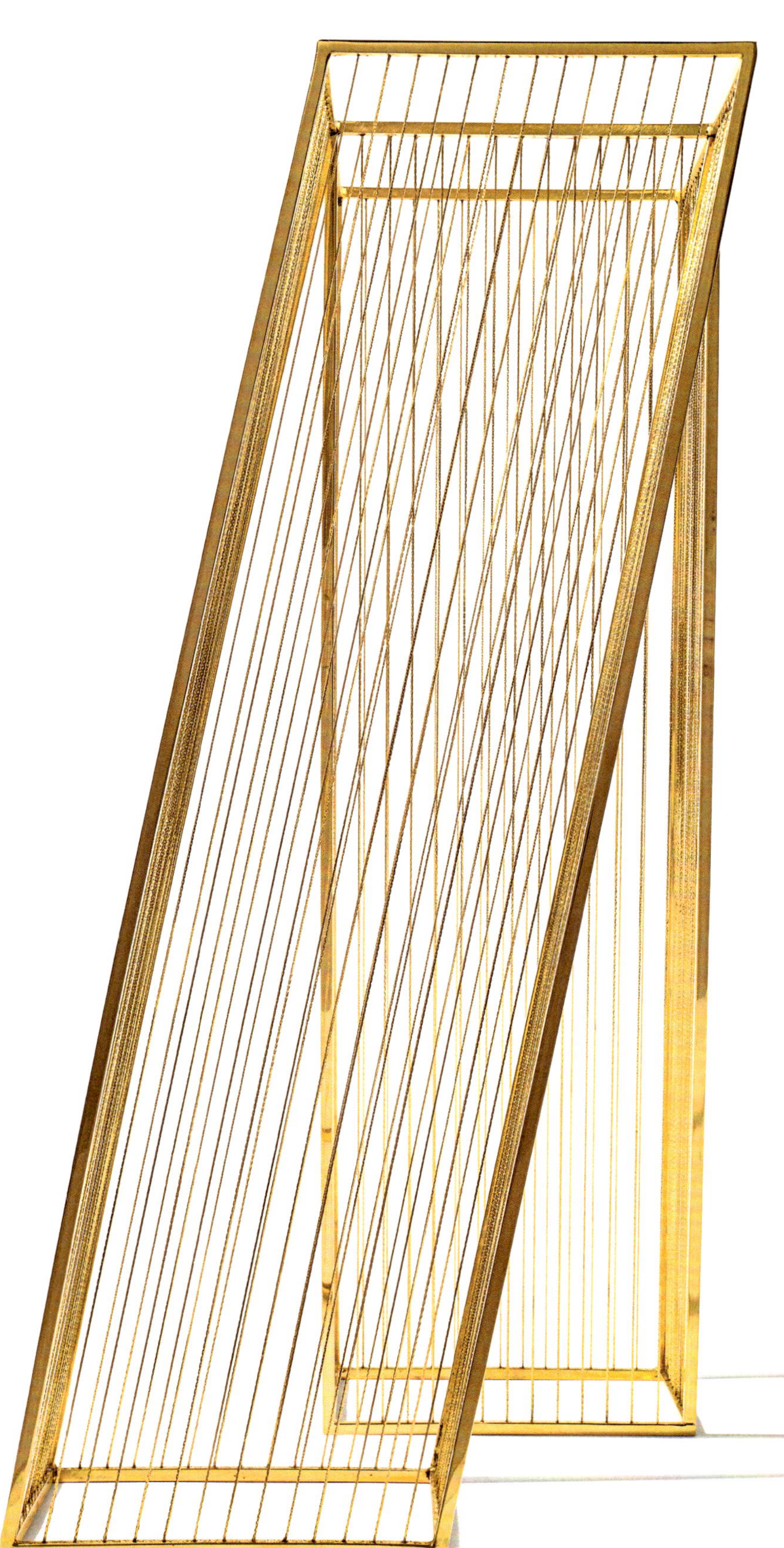

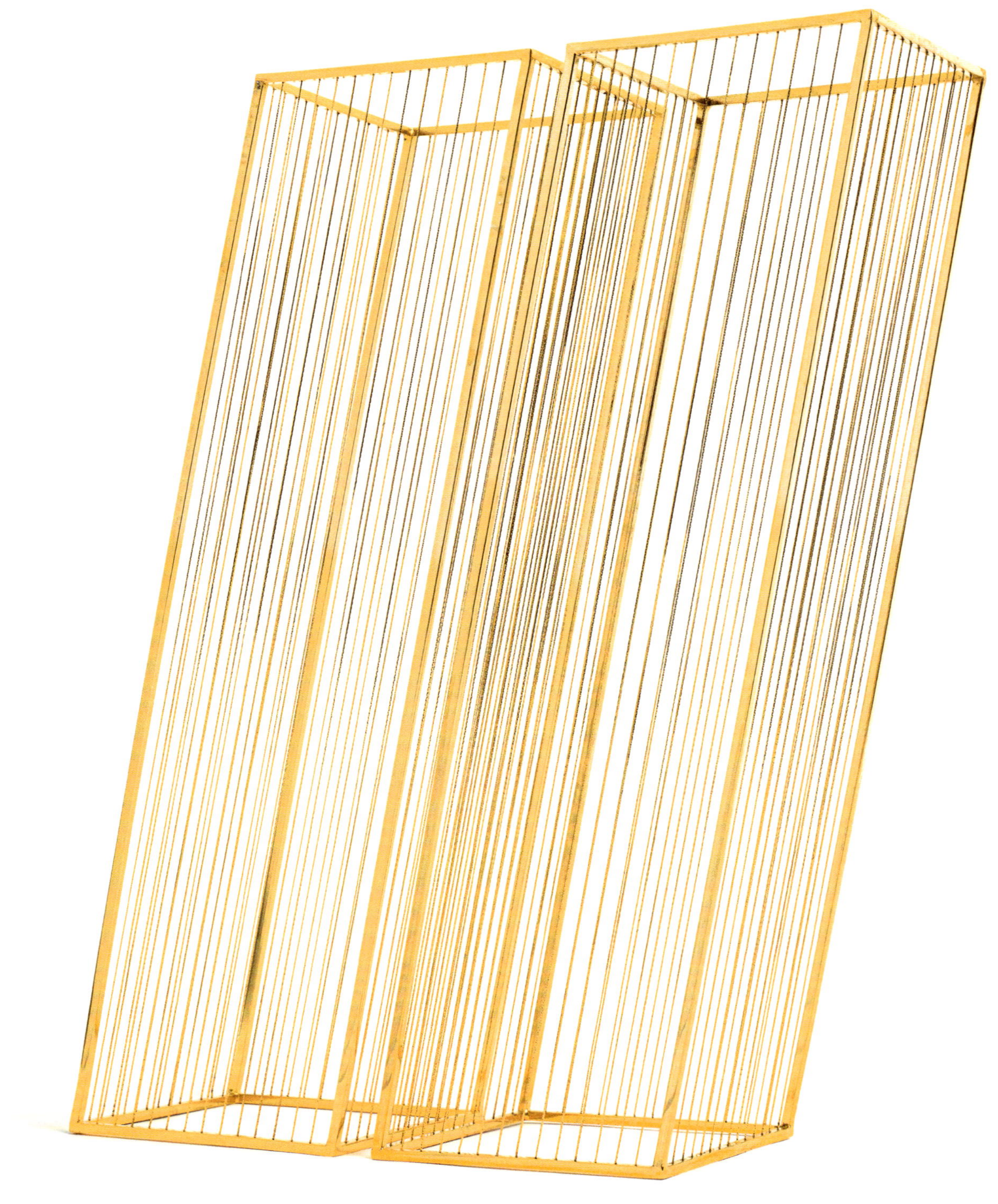

Ttéia 1, C, Metallic #5, 2003

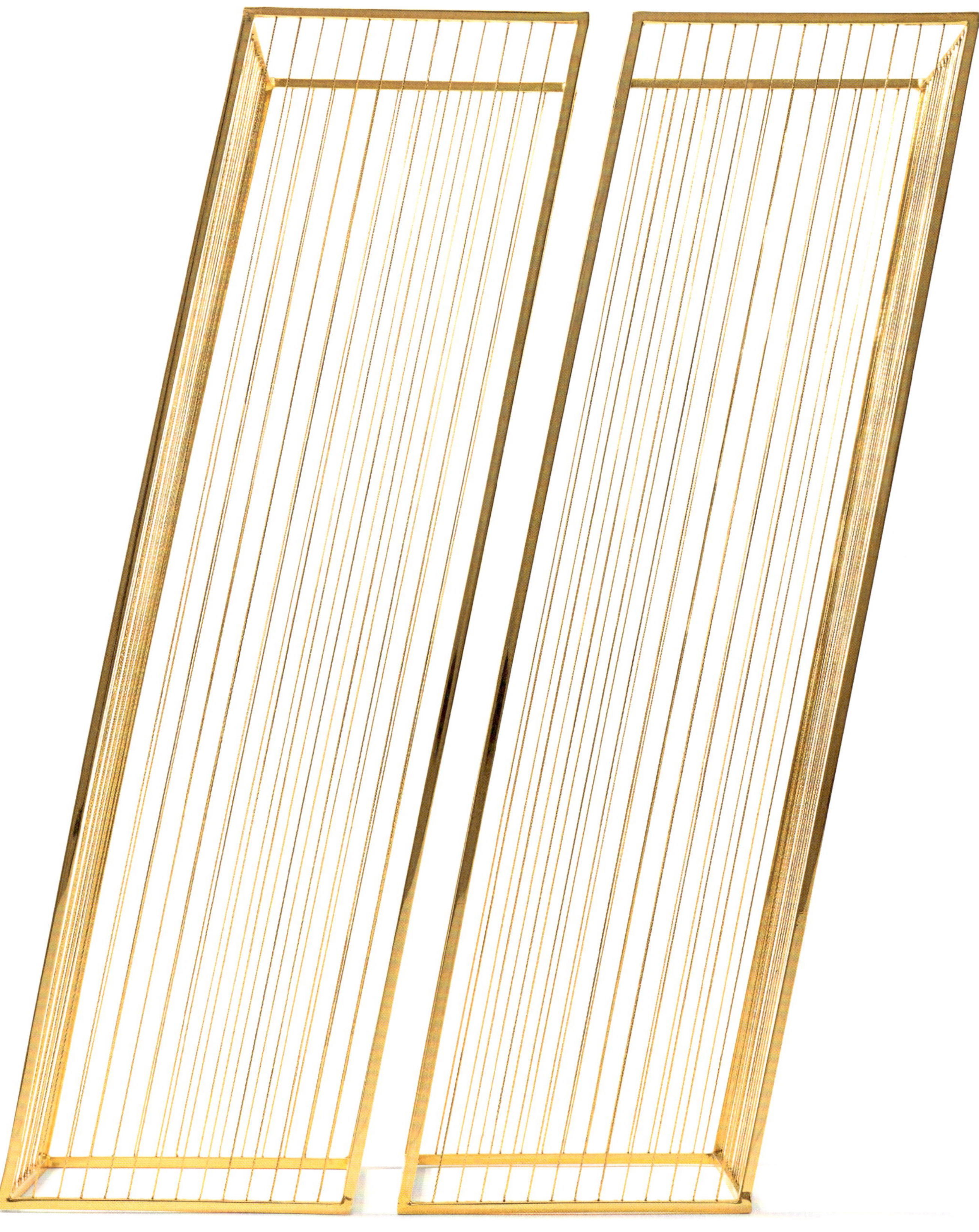

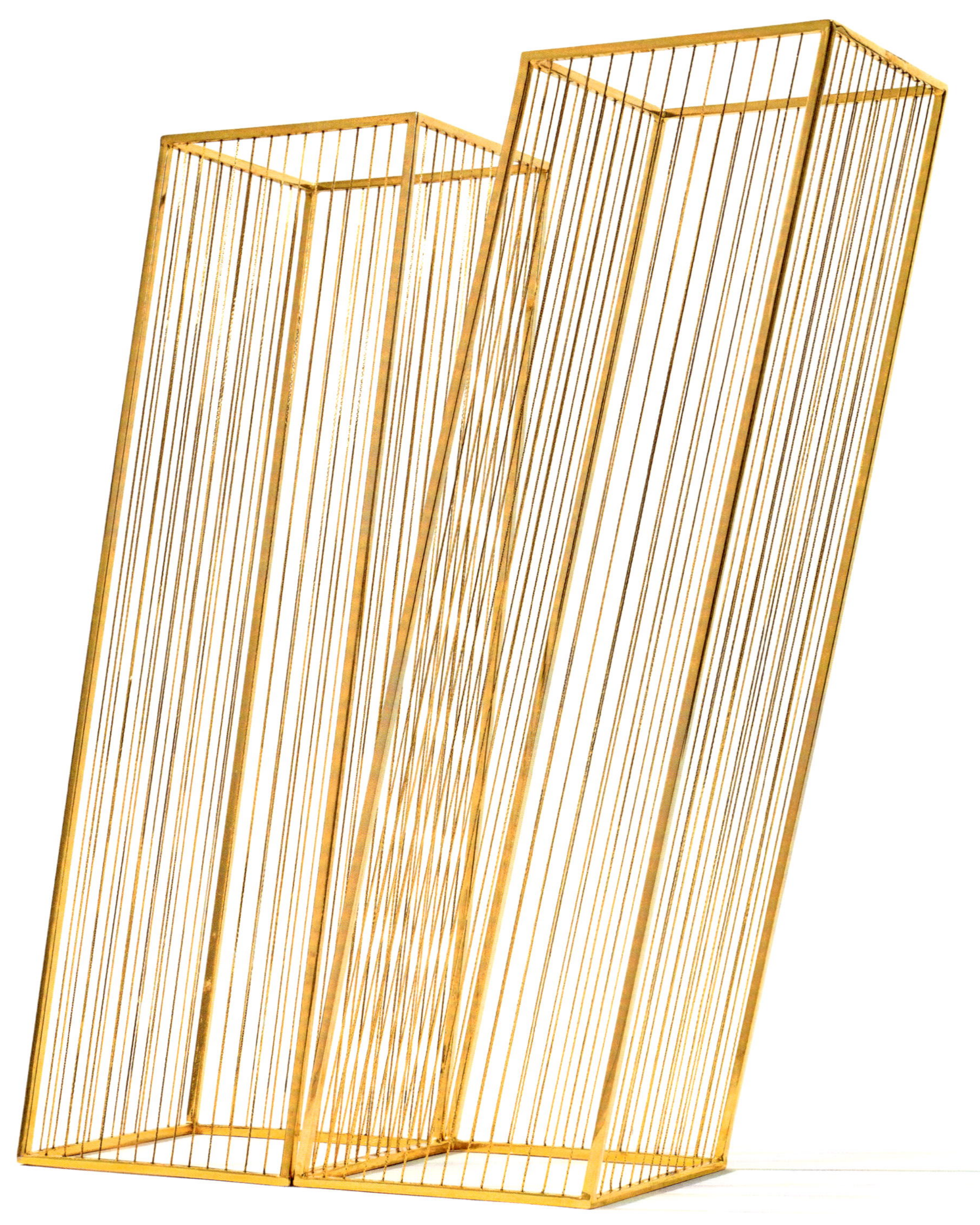

Ttéia 1, C, Metallic #6, 2003

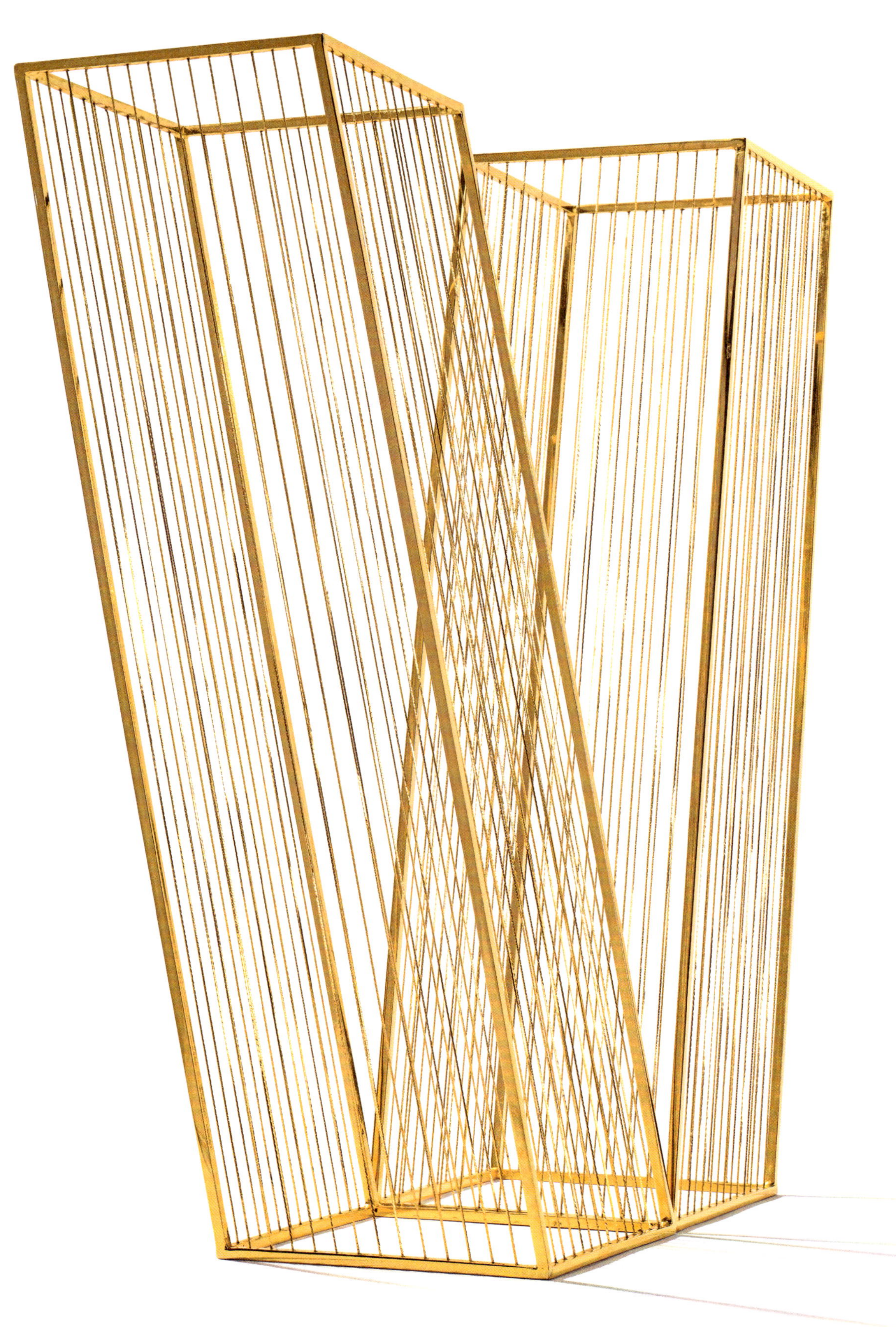

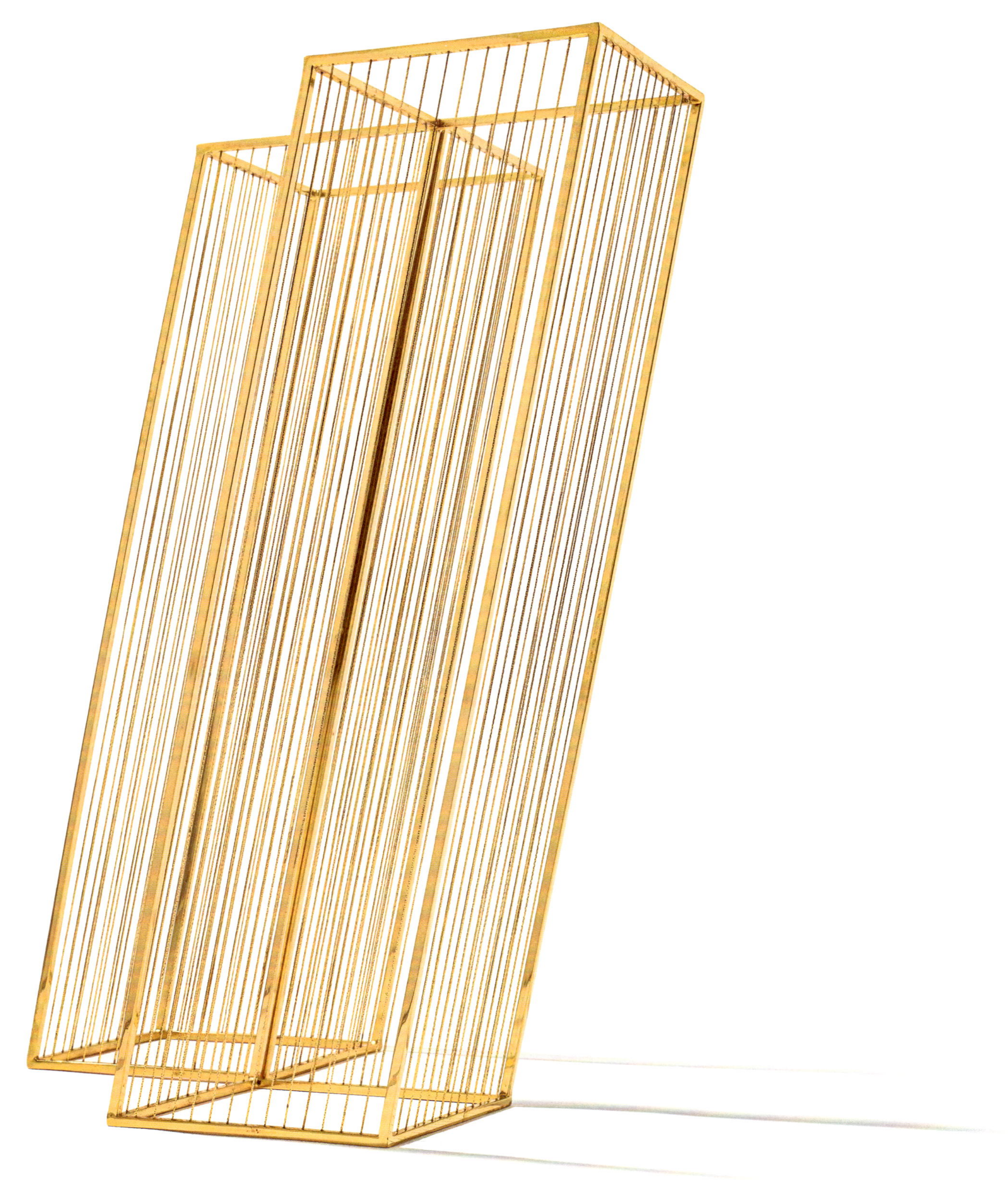

Ttéia 1, C, Metallic #8, 2003

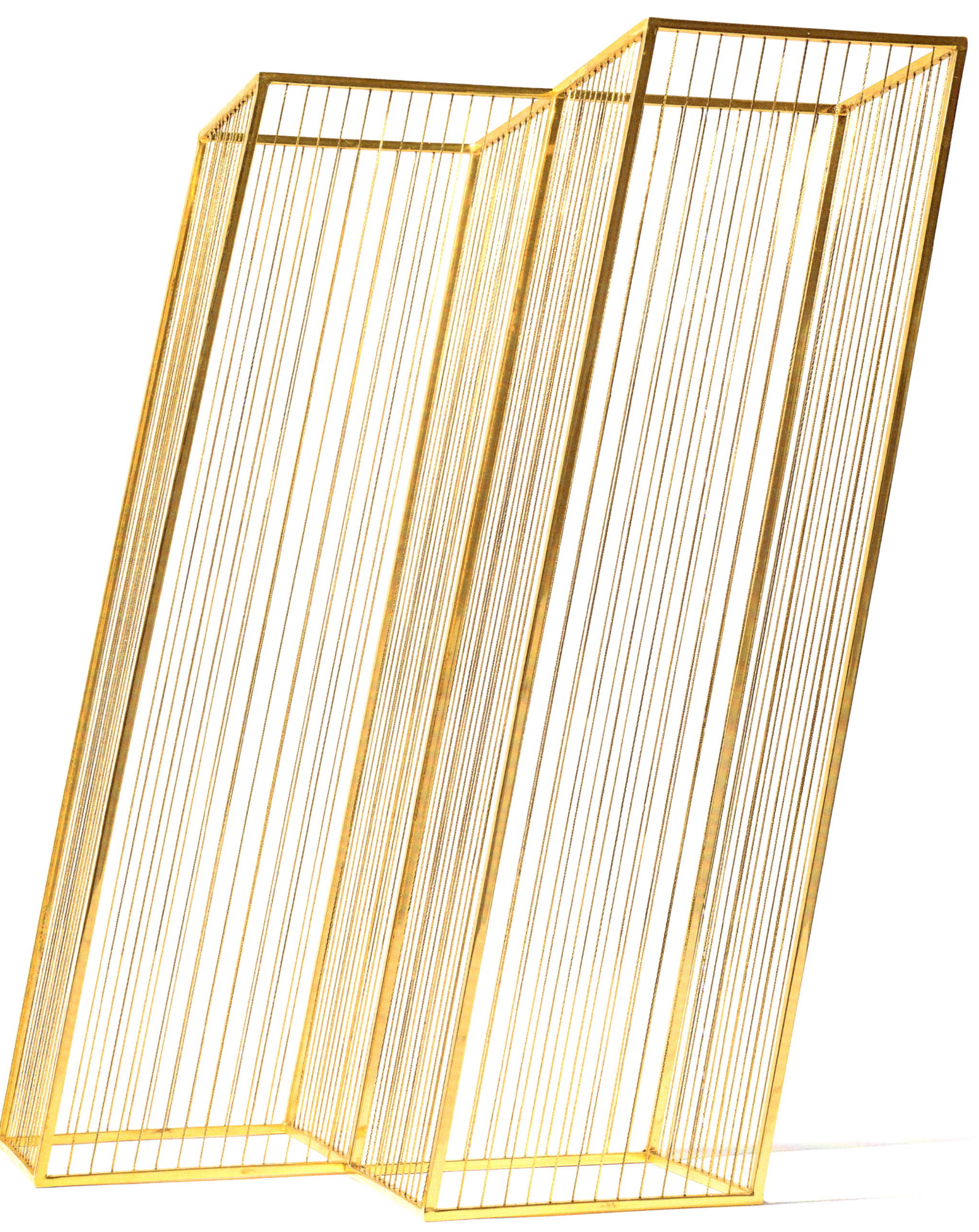

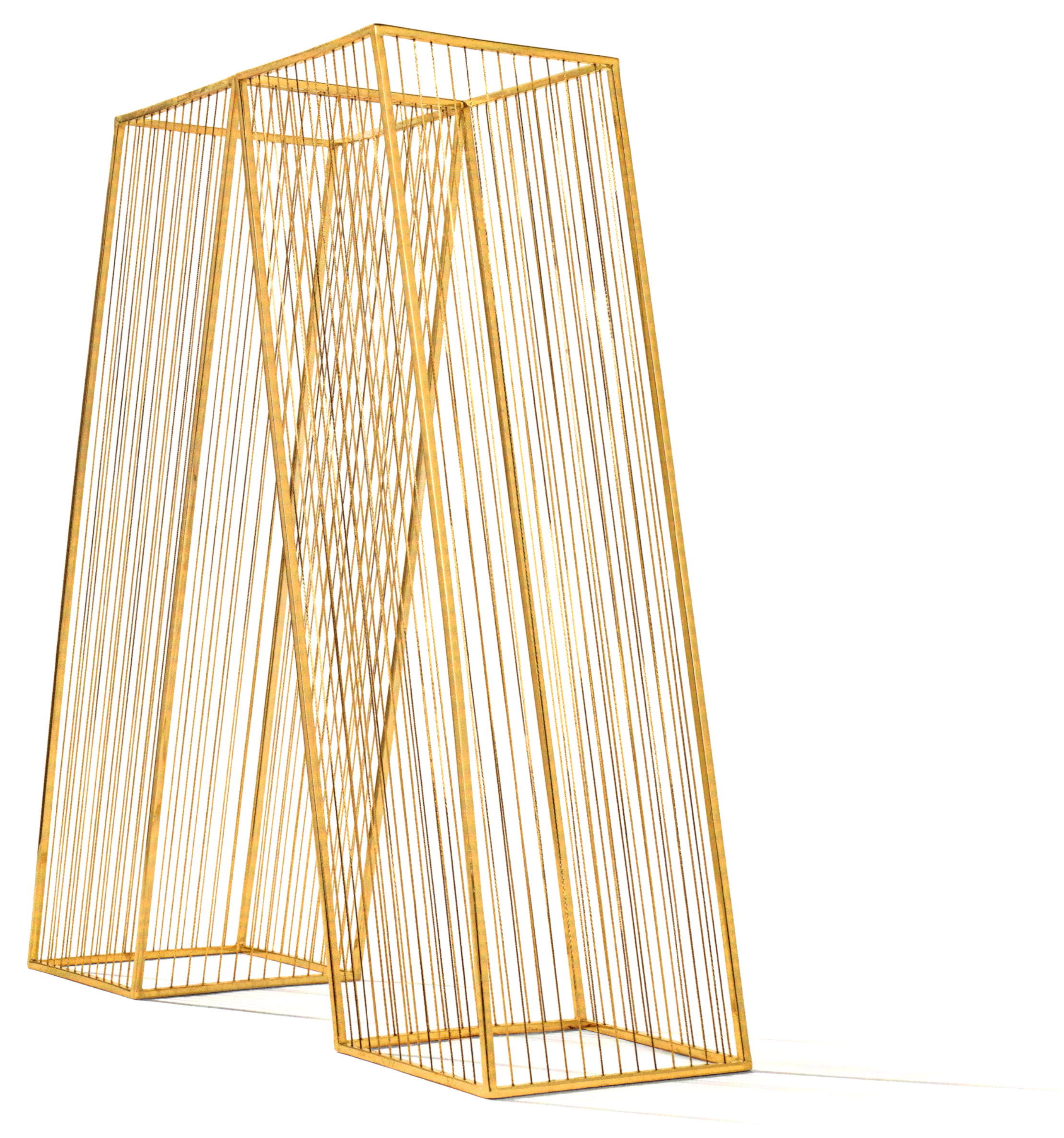

Ttéia 1, C, Metallic #9, 2003

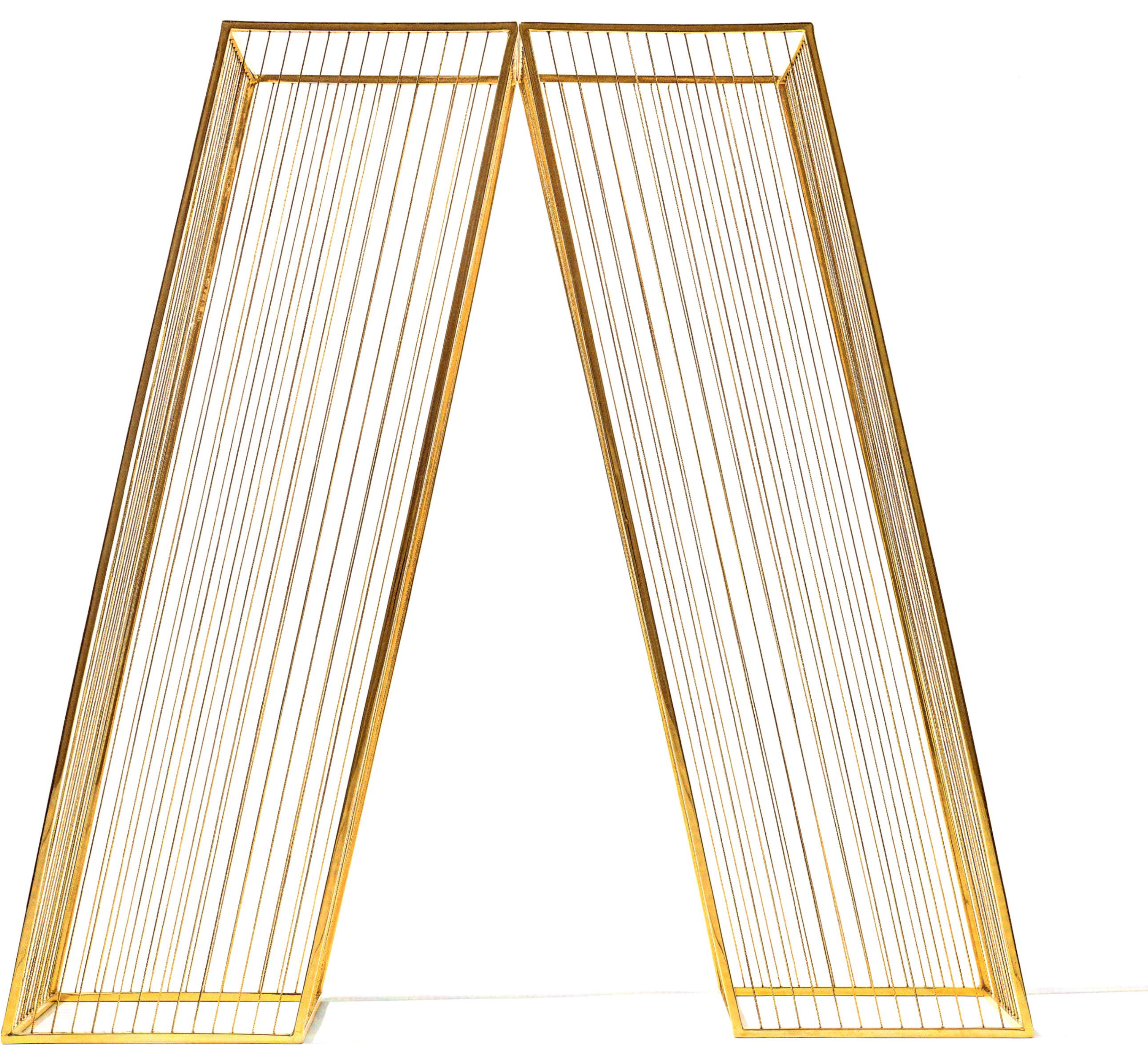

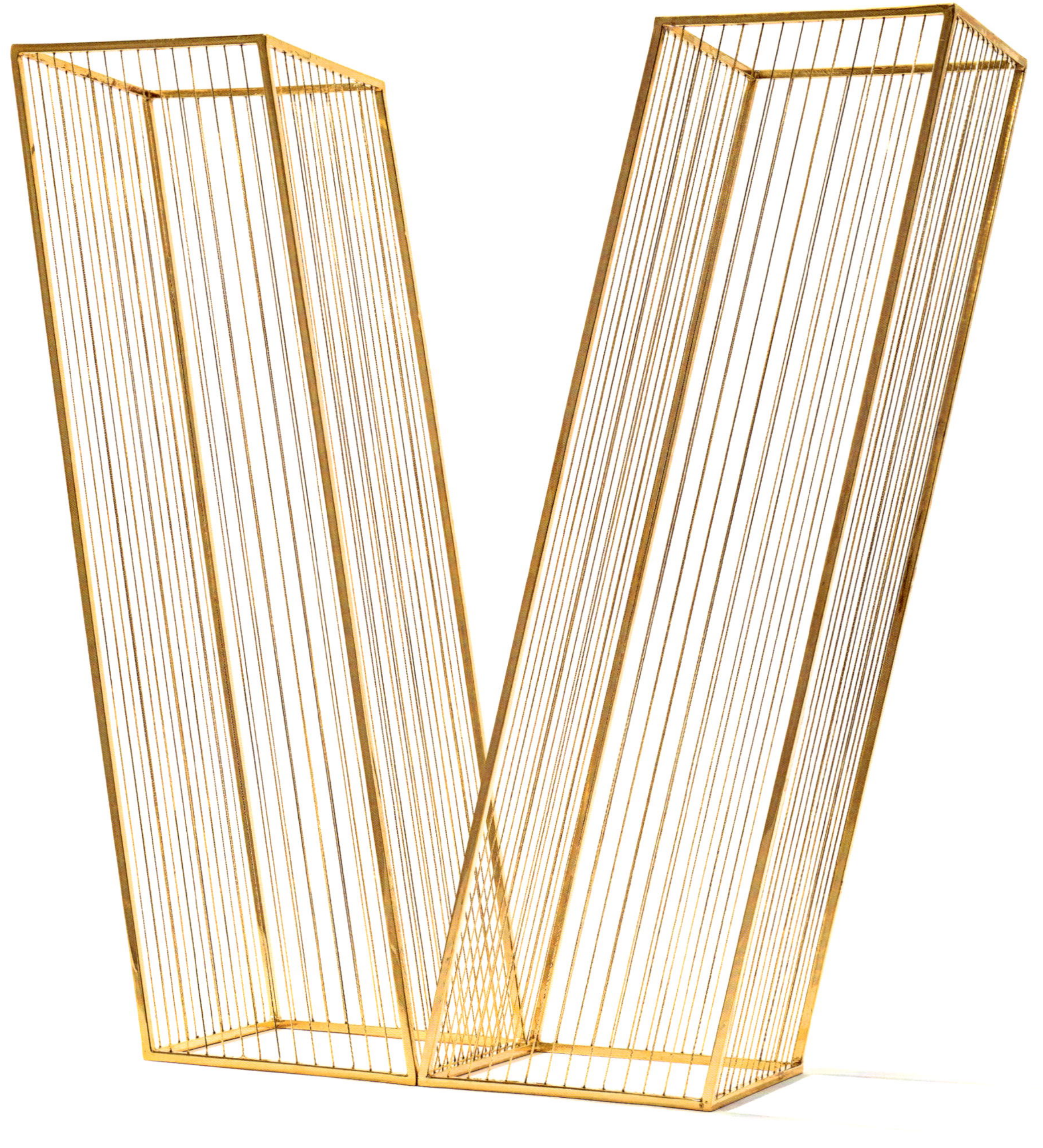

Ttéia 1, C, Metallic #10, 2003

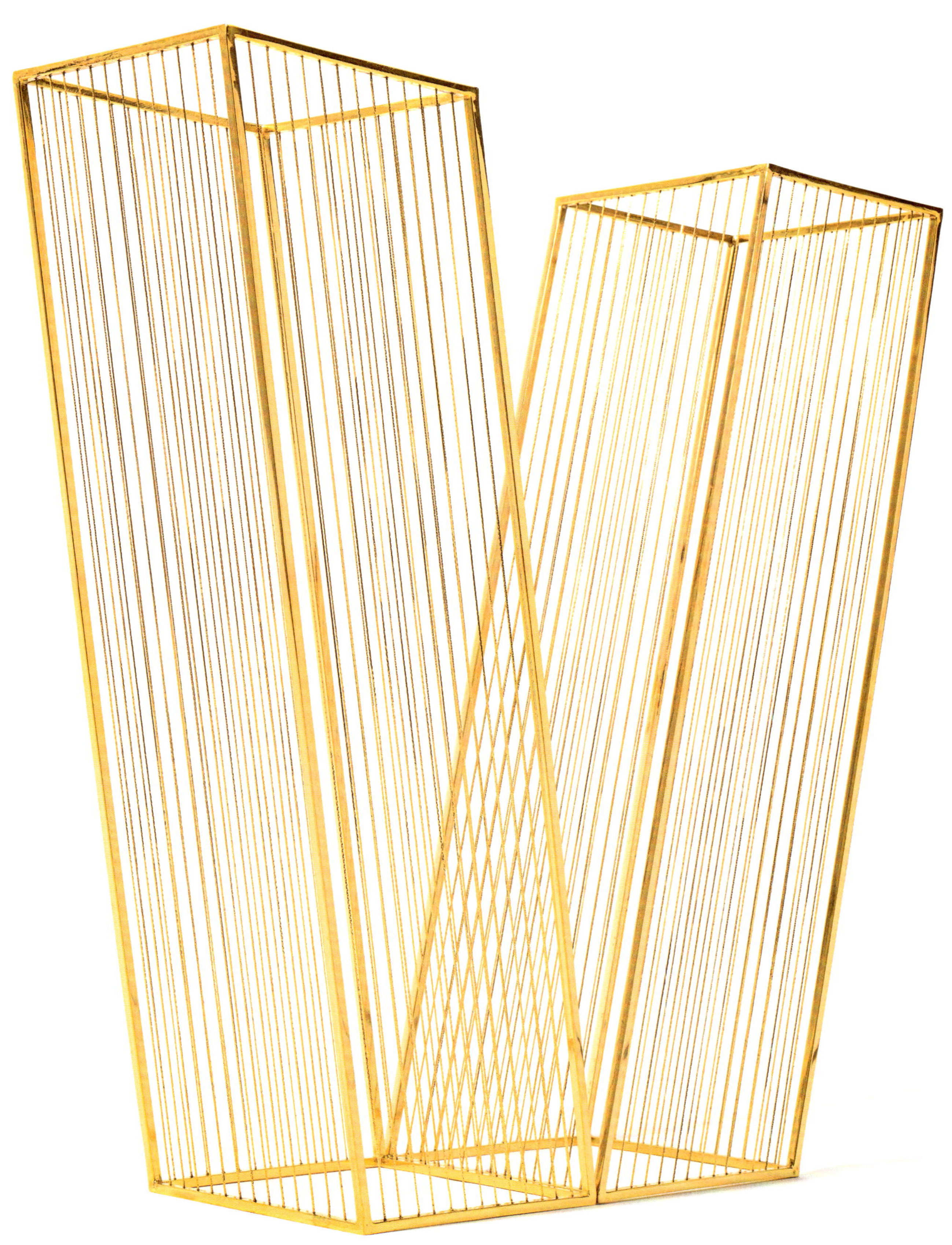

Ttéia 1, A, 1978/1979/1991

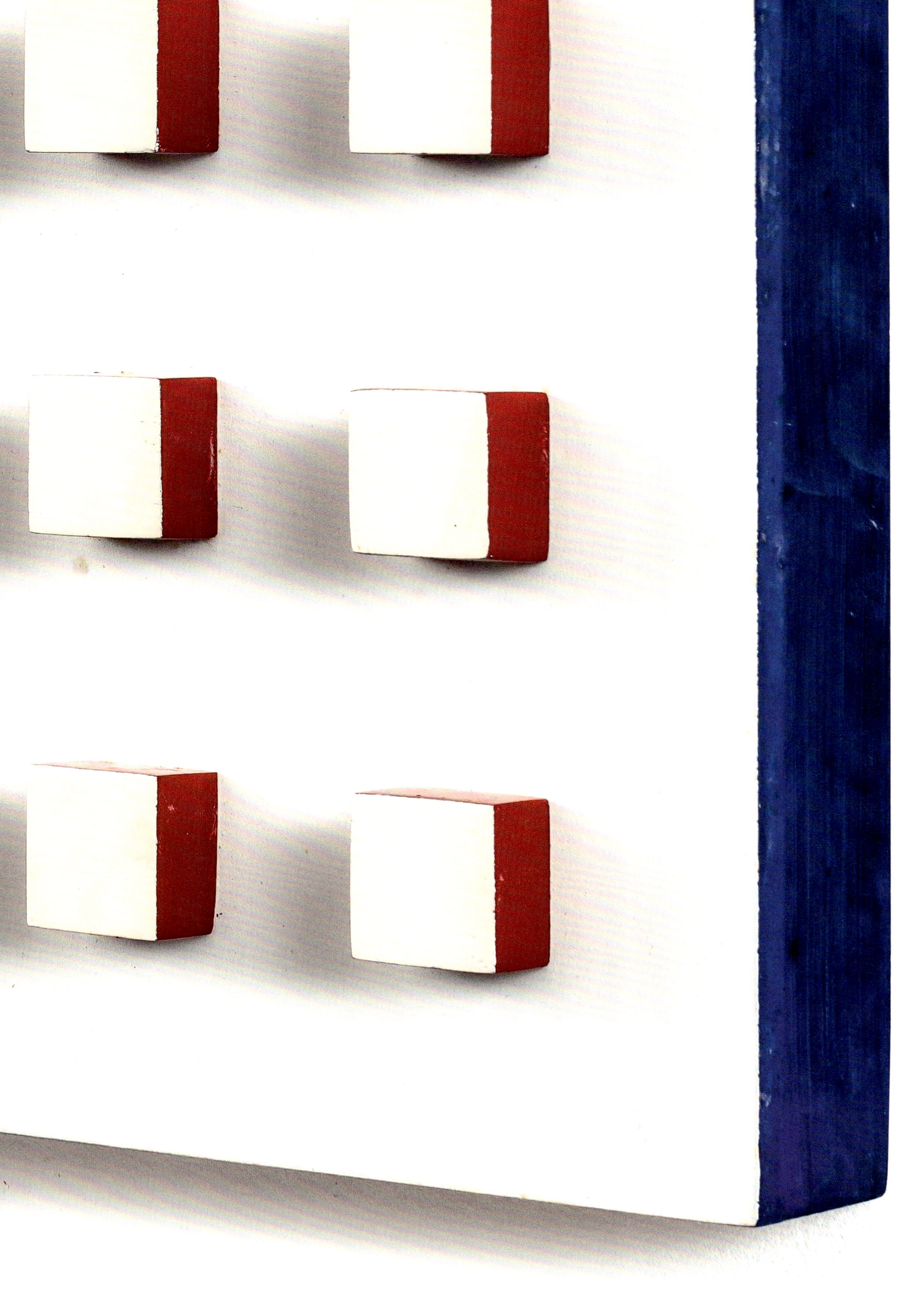

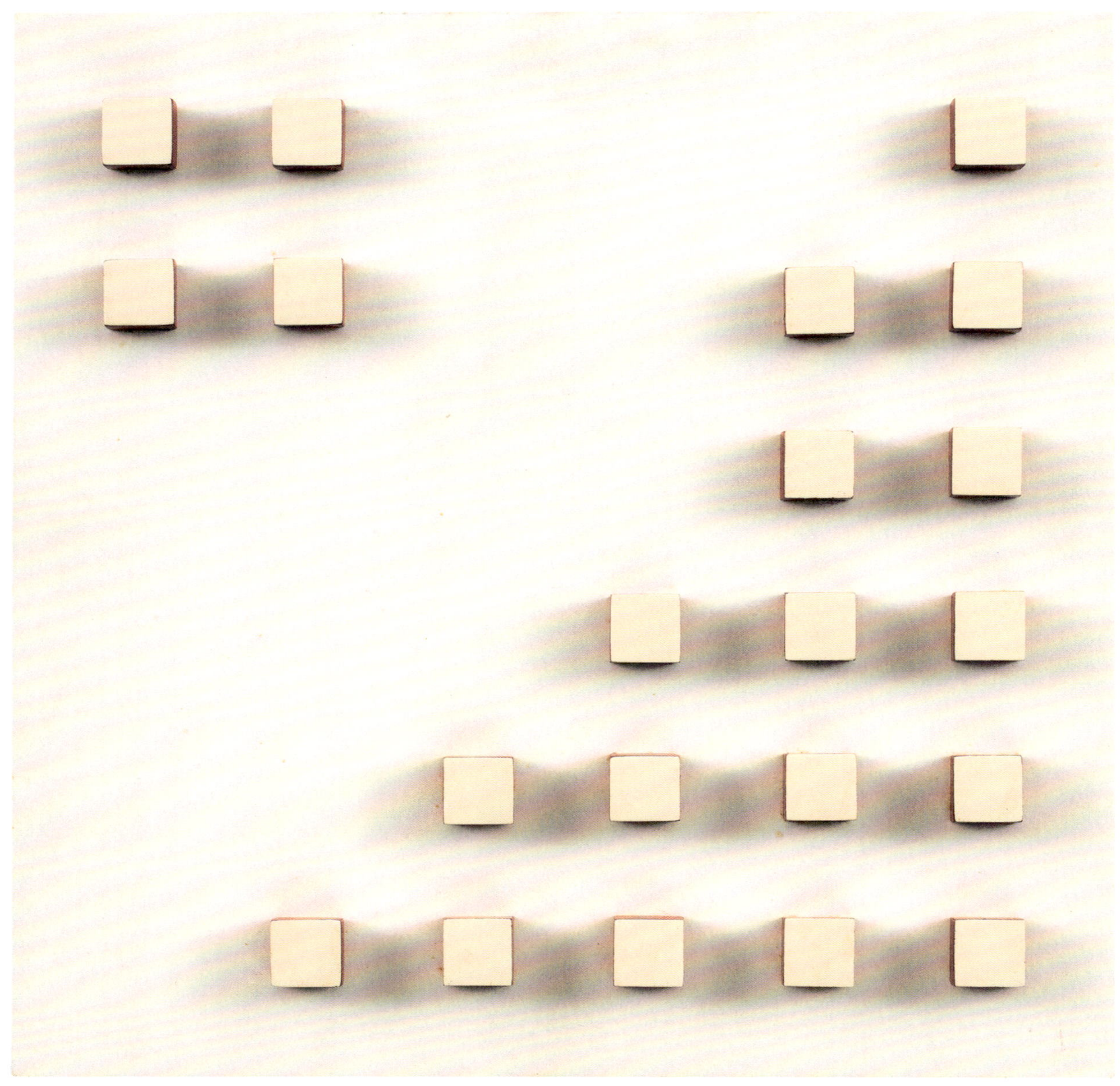

134—135   *Relevo* (Relief), 1954/1956

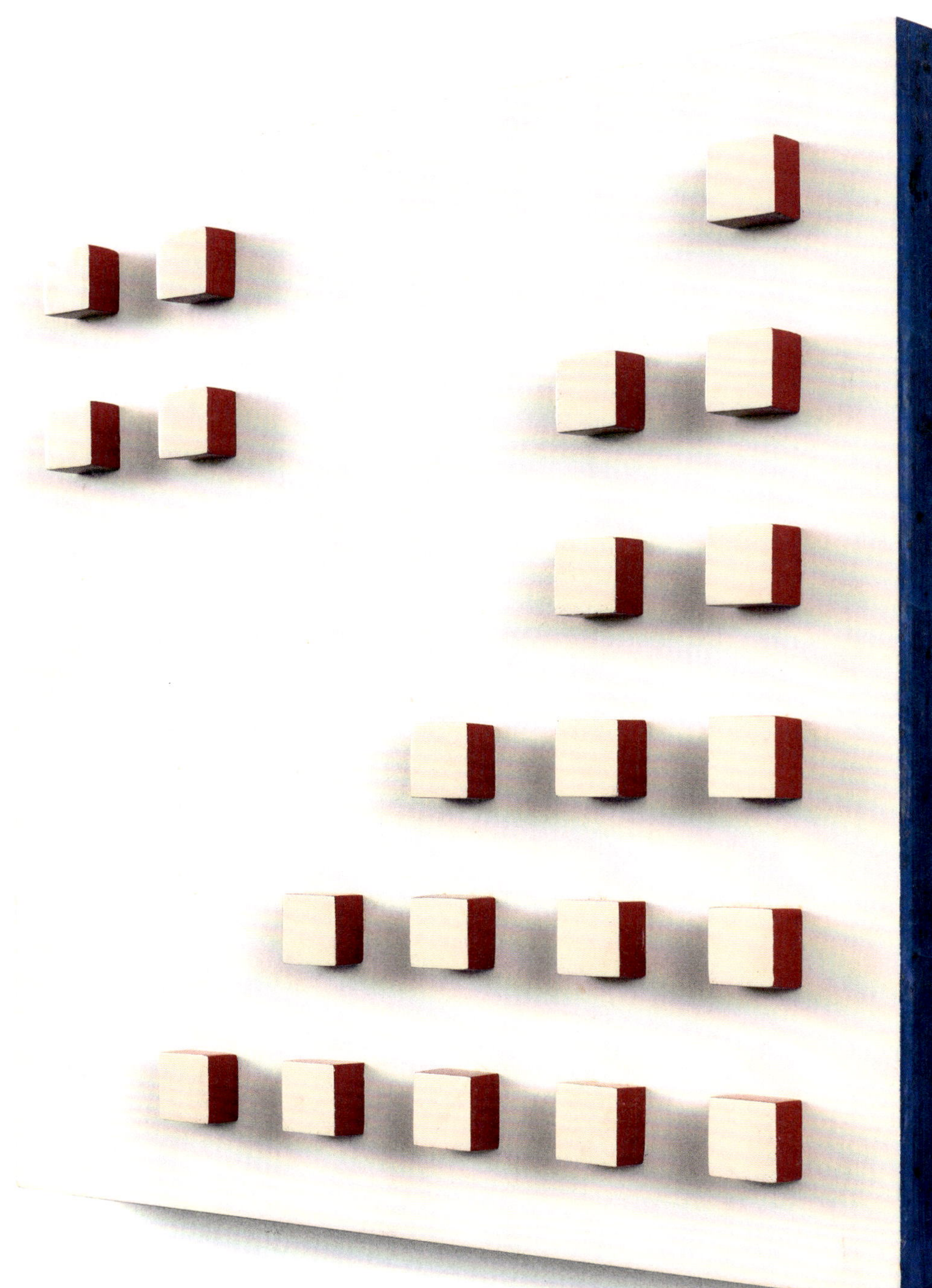

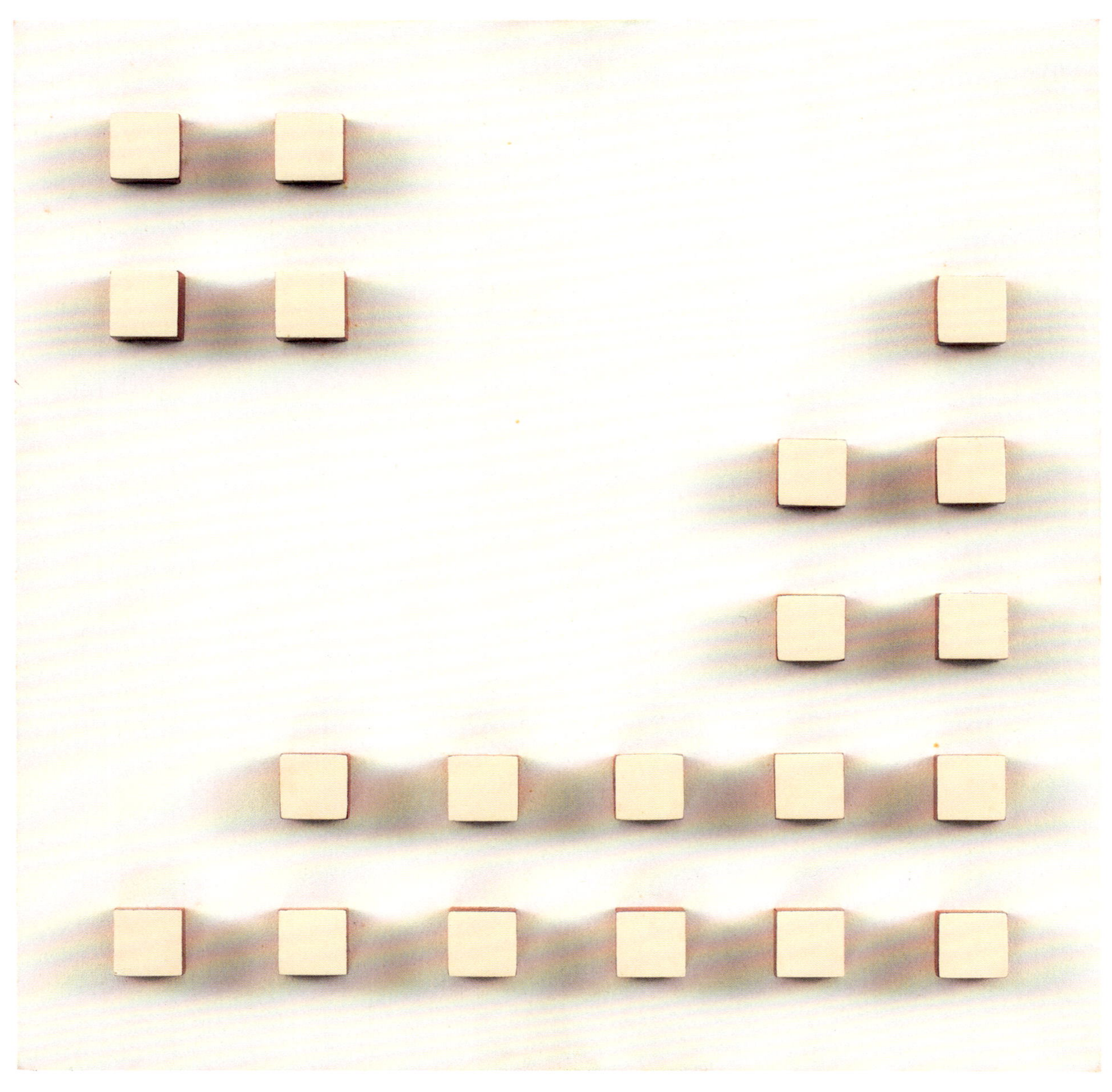

Relevo (Relief), 1954/1956

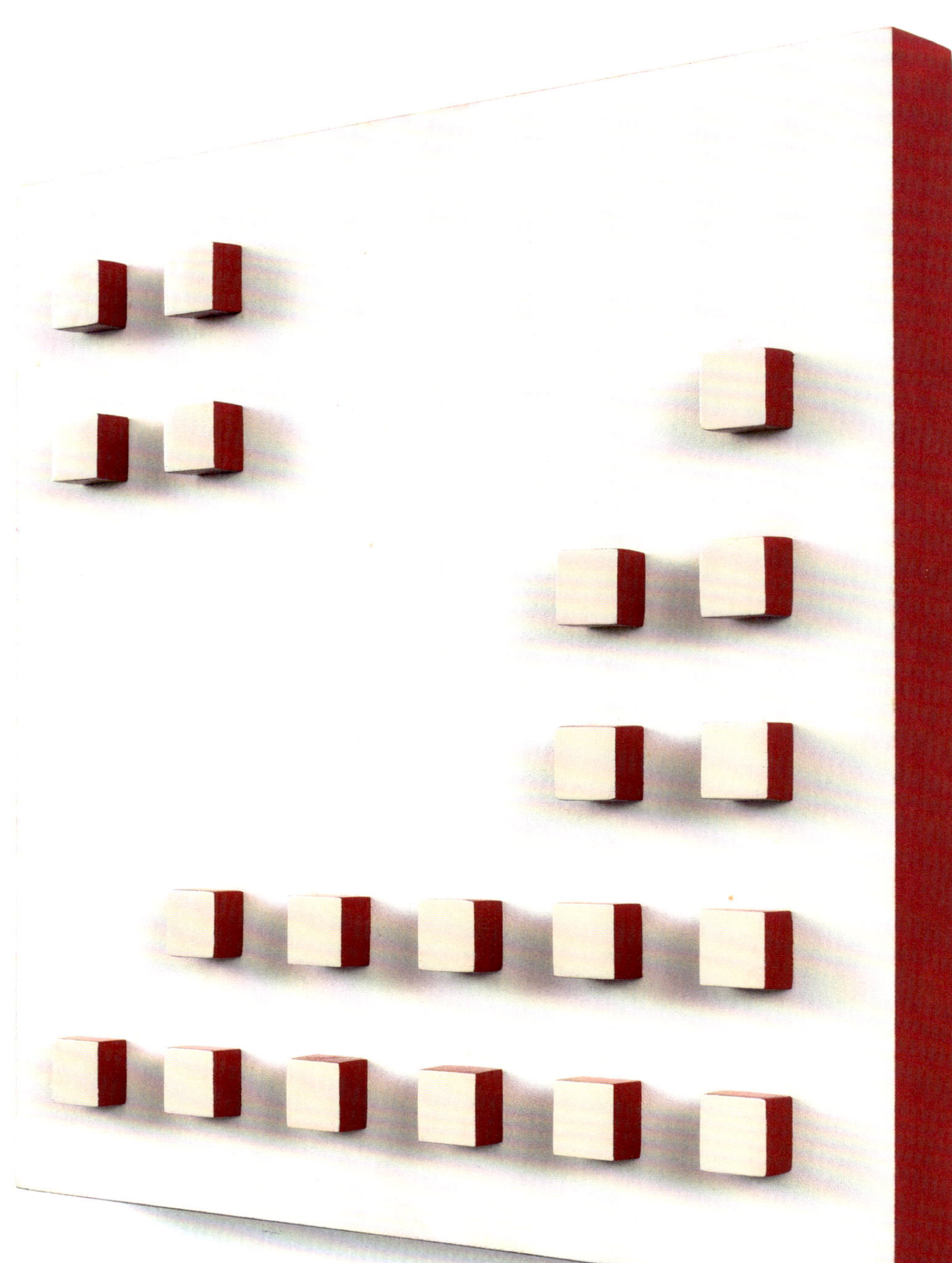

List of Works

Amazonino Vermelho
(Red Amazonino)
1989/2003
Automotive paint on iron
47 ½ × 19 ¾ × 45 ¼ in.
120.7 × 50.2 × 114.9 cm
pp. 20 (fig. 7), 70, 71

Amazonino Vermelho
(Red Amazonino)
1989/2003
Automotive paint on iron
34 ¼ × 19 ¾ × 21 ¼ in.
87 × 50.2 × 54 cm
pp. 21 (fig. 8), 88, 89

Amazonino Vermelho
(Red Amazonino)
1989/2003
Automotive paint on iron
26 ¾ × 19 ¾ × 21 ½ in.
67.9 × 50.2 × 54.6 cm
pp. 72, 73

Amazonino Vermelho
(Red Amazonino)
1989/2003
Automotive paint on iron
19 ¾ × 19 ¾ × 6 ½ in.
50.2 × 50.2 × 16.5 cm
pp. 74, 75

Amazonino Vermelho
(Red Amazonino)
1989/2003
Automotive paint on iron
19 ¾ × 19 ¾ × 6 ¾ in.
50.2 × 50.2 × 17 cm
pp. 76, 77

Amazonino Vermelho
(Red Amazonino)
1989/2003
Automotive paint on iron
21 ⅞ × 19 ¾ × 11 ⅜ in.
55.6 × 50.2 × 28.9 cm
pp. 78 (detail), 79

Amazonino Vermelho
(Red Amazonino)
1989/2003
Automotive paint on iron
21 × 19 ¾ × 8 ¼ in.
53.3 × 50.2 × 21 cm
pp. 80, 81

Amazonino Vermelho
(Red Amazonino)
1989/2003
Automotive paint on iron
51 ¼ × 19 ⅝ × 27 in.
130.2 × 49.8 × 68.6 cm
pp. 82 (detail), 83

Amazonino Vermelho
(Red Amazonino)
1989/2003
Automotive paint on iron
19 ¾ × 19 ¾ × 6 ½ in.
50.2 × 50.2 × 16.5 cm
pp. 84, 85

Amazonino Vermelho
(Red Amazonino)
1989/2003
Automotive paint on iron
47 ½ × 19 ¾ × 45 ¼ in.
120.7 × 50.2 × 114.9 cm
pp. 86 (detail), 87

Amazonino Vermelho
(Red Amazonino)
1989/2003
Automotive paint on iron
19 ¾ × 19 ¾ × 6 ⅝ in.
50.2 × 50.2 × 16.7 cm
pp. 90, 91

Amazonino Vermelho
(Red Amazonino)
1989/2003
Automotive paint on iron
19 ¾ × 19 ¾ × 6 ½ in.
50.2 × 50.2 × 16.4 cm
pp. 92, 93

Amazonino Vermelho
(Red Amazonino)
1989/2003
Automotive paint on iron
21 × 19 ¾ × 8 ¼ in.
53.3 × 50.2 × 21 cm
p. 94, 95

Amazonino Vermelho
(Red Amazonino)
1989/2003
Automotive paint on iron
21 ¾ × 19 ¾ × 11 ⅜ in.
55.3 × 50.2 × 29 cm
pp. 96, 97

Amazonino Vermelho
(Red Amazonino)
1989/2003
Automotive paint on iron
22 ½ × 19 ¾ × 17 in.
57.2 × 50.2 × 43.2 cm
pp. 98, 99

Amazonino Vermelho
(Red Amazonino)
1989/2003
Automotive paint on iron
19 ¾ × 19 ¾ × 6 ⅜ in.
50.2 × 50.2 × 16.2 cm
pp. 100, 101

Amazonino Vermelho
(Red Amazonino)
1989/2003
Automotive paint on iron
20 ⅞ × 19 ¾ × 6 ½ in.
53 × 50.2 × 16.5 cm
p. 102

*Amazonino Vermelho
e Preto* (Red and Black
Amazonino)
1990
Automotive paint on iron
126 × 110 ⅜ × 36 in.
320 × 280.5 × 91.4 cm
pp. 4 (detail), 67, 68
(detail), 69

Desenho (Drawing)
1956
White ink on Japanese
paper
8 ¼ × 7 in.
20.8 × 17.8 cm
p. 49

Desenho (Drawing)
1956
White ink on
Japanese paper
12 ⅞ × 8 ⅞ in.
32.7 × 22.4 cm
p. 51

Desenho (Drawing)
1956
White ink on
Japanese paper
23 ⅞ × 19 ¼ in.
60.8 × 48.9 cm
p. 53

Desenho (Drawing)
1956
White ink on
Japanese paper
9 ½ × 7 ¾ in.
24 × 19.8 cm
p. 55

Jogo de Ténis
(Tennis Game)
2001
Video installation
Dimensions variable
p. 64 (film still)

Mineiro (Miner)
1968
Color photograph
75 ⅞ × 58 ⅝ in.
192.7 × 148.9 cm
p. 19 (fig. 6)

Objeto de Sedução
(Object of Seduction)
1970
Collage, mixed media
on paper
14 ½ × 21 ⅝ in.
36.8 × 55 cm
p. 57

Objeto de Sedução
(Object of Seduction)
1970
Collage, mixed media
on paper
14 ½ × 21 ⅝ in.
36.7 × 54.9 cm
p. 59

Relevo (Relief)
1954/1956
Automotive paint and
tempera on wood
15 ¾ × 15 ¾ × 2 in.
40 × 40 × 5 cm
pp. 133 (detail), 134, 135

Relevo (Relief)
1954/1956
Automotive paint and
tempera on wood
15 ¾ × 15 ¾ × 2 in.
40 × 40 × 5 cm
pp. 136, 137

Roda dos prazeres
(Wheel of Pleasures)
1967
Porcelain vessels,
droppers, water,
flavorings, food dyes
Dimensions variable
Installation view,
the artist's house,
Rio de Janeiro, 1992
p. 18 (fig. 5)

Tecelar
1952
Woodcut print on
Japanese paper
12 ¾ × 17 ⅝ in.
32.5 × 44.9 cm
p. 27

Tecelar
1953
Woodcut print on
Japanese paper
12 ¾ × 17 ⅝ in.
32.5 × 44.9 cm
p. 10 (fig. 1)

Tecelar
1953
Woodcut print on
Japanese paper
17 ½ × 13 in.
44.5 × 33 cm
p. 33

Tecelar
1953
Woodcut print on
Japanese paper
17 ⅝ × 15 in.
44.7 × 38 cm
p. 35

Tecelar
1953
Woodcut print on
Japanese paper
25 ⅝ × 17 ⅝ in.
65 × 44.7 cm
p. 36

Tecelar
1953
Woodcut print on
Japanese paper
17 ½ × 13 in.
44.4 × 32.9 cm
p. 37

Tecelar
1954
Woodcut print on
Japanese paper
15 ⅞ × 12 ⅞ in.
40.2 × 32.7 cm
p. 29

*Tecelar**
c. 1955
Woodcut print on
Japanese paper
12 × 9 in.
30.5 × 23 cm
p. 11 (fig. 2)

Tecelar
1955
Woodcut print on
Japanese paper
19 ¼ × 23 ⅞ in.
49 × 60.5 cm
p. 13 (fig. 3)

Tecelar
1955
Woodcut print on
Japanese paper
17 ½ × 12 ⅞ in.
44.3 × 32.7 cm
p. 31

Tecelar
1955
Woodcut print on
Japanese paper
25 ⅝ × 22 ⅞ in.
65 × 58 cm
p. 41

Tecelar
1955
Woodcut print on
Japanese paper
23 ⅞ × 16 ⅝ in.
60.8 × 42.2 cm
p. 42

Tecelar
1955
Woodcut print on
Japanese paper
24 ⅛ × 15 ½ in.
61.3 × 39.5 cm
p. 43

Tecelar
1957
Woodcut print on
Japanese paper
18 ⅜ × 17 ⅞ in.
46.7 × 45.5 cm
p. 39

Tecelar
1958
Woodcut print on
Japanese paper
18 × 17 ½ in.
45.8 × 44.5 cm
p. 45

Tecelar
1958
Woodcut print on
Japanese paper
12 ⅞ × 11 ¾ in.
32.7 × 29.7 cm
p. 47

Tecelar
1959
Woodcut print on
Japanese paper
11 ¾ × 21 ¼ in.
30 × 54 cm
p. 14 (fig. 4)

Tecelar
1959
Woodcut print on
Japanese paper
9 ⅝ × 11 ¾ in.
24.6 × 29.7 cm
p. 46

Ttéia 1, A
1978/1979/1991
Silver thread, nails, light
118 ⅛ × 70 ⅞ × 35 ⅜ in.
300 × 180 × 90 cm
p. 131

*Ttéia 1, C**
2001/2016
Silver thread, wood, nails,
light
Dimensions variable
Installation view, *Lygia
Pape*, Hauser & Wirth
London, 2016
p. 22 (fig. 9)

Ttéia 1, C, Metallic #1
2003
Gold-plated copper
19 ¼ × 13 ¼ × 11 ¼ in.
48.9 × 33.7 × 28.6 cm
pp. 111 (detail), 112, 113

Ttéia 1, C, Metallic #2
2003
Gold-plated copper
19 ¼ × 10 ⅞ × 11 in.
49 × 27.5 × 28 cm
pp. 114, 115

Ttéia 1, C, Metallic #3
2003
Gold-plated copper
19 ¼ × 13 ¼ × 11 in.
48.9 × 33.7 × 27.9 cm
pp. 116, 117

Ttéia 1, C, Metallic #4
2003
Gold-plated copper
19 ¼ × 9 ¼ × 11 in.
49 × 23.5 × 28 cm
pp. 118, 119

Ttéia 1, C, Metallic #5
2003
Gold-plated copper
19 ¼ × 16 × 5 ½ in.
49 × 40.6 × 14 cm
pp. 120, 121

Ttéia 1, C, Metallic #6
2003
Gold-plated copper
19 ¼ × 9 ¼ × 14 ¼ in.
49 × 23.5 × 36.2 cm
pp. 122, 123

Ttéia 1, C, Metallic #8
2003
Gold-plated copper
19 ½ × 14 ½ × 11 in.
49.5 × 36.8 × 27.9 cm
pp. 124, 125

Ttéia 1, C, Metallic #9
2003
Gold-plated copper
19 ¼ × 18 ⅛ × 5 ½ in.
49 × 46 × 14 cm
pp. 126, 127

Ttéia 1, C, Metallic #10
2003
Gold-plated copper
19 ¼ × 18 ½ × 5 ½ in.
49 × 47 × 14 cm
pp. 128, 129

Untitled collage by Lygia
Pape and Ivan Serpa
1972
Collage, mixed media
on paper
19 ⅝ × 19 ⅝ in.
49.8 × 49.8 cm
p. 61

Untitled collage by Lygia
Pape and Ivan Serpa
1972
Collage, mixed media
on paper
19 ⅝ × 19 ⅝ in.
49.8 × 49.8 cm
p. 63

* Not in the exhibition

Lygia Pape
1927–2004
Lived and worked in Rio de Janeiro

A member of Grupo Frente and one of the signatories of the "Neoconcrete Manifesto" (1959), Lygia Pape worked at the forefront of the Brazilian avant-garde. She began exhibiting in the early 1950s and received a master's degree in philosophy from the Universidade Federal do Rio de Janeiro in 1980. Her work has been the subject of important solo exhibitions on an international scale, most recently the travelling retrospective *Magnetized Space* at Museo Nacional Centro de Arte Reina Sofía, Madrid (2011), Serpentine Gallery, London (2011), and Pinacoteca do Estado de São Paulo (2012); and including a presentation at Museu de Arte Contemporânea de Serralves, Porto (2000). Her piece *Ttéia 1, C* was featured in the 53rd Venice Biennale (2009), where it earned Special Mention. In 2017 *Lygia Pape: A Multitude of Forms*, the first major retrospective in the United States devoted to her work, was presented at The Metropolitan Museum of Art, New York.

Alexander Alberro is the Virginia Wright Professor of Modern and Contemporary Art History at Barnard College and Columbia University. His most recent book, *Abstraction in Reverse: The Reconfigured Spectator in Mid-Twentieth Century Latin American Art*, is published by University of Chicago Press. He has also written and edited numerous volumes on contemporary art, and contributed essays to a broad array of critical journals and exhibition catalogs.

Paulo Herkenhoff is an art historian, critic, and independent curator. His writing has been published by such international art institutions as Tate Modern (London), Centre Georges Pompidou (Paris), and The Fogg Art Museum Harvard (where he announced the "Law of Lygia Pape"). In 2011 he contributed an essay "Lygia Pape: The Art of Passage" to the exhibition catalog of *Magnetized Space* at the Reina Sofía, Madrid. Herkenhoff was curator of the Brazilian Pavilion at the 41st (1984) and 47th (1997) Venice Biennales, and art director of the 24th São Paulo Biennial (1998). He first met Lygia Pape in 1969 and as chief curator of the Museu de Arte Moderna do Rio de Janeiro (MAM-RJ, 1985–90), he acquired a number of *Tecelares* for their collection. Herkenhoff has held positions as adjunct curator in the Department of Painting and Sculpture, MoMA, New York (1999–2002); director at the Museu Nacional de Belas Artes, Rio de Janeiro (2003–6); and artistic director of the Museu de Arte do Rio (MAR, 2011–16).

Ferreira Gullar (1930–2016), born José Ribamar Ferreira, was a Brazilian poet, art critic, essayist, and dramatist. Along with Lygia Pape, Lygia Clark, Hélio Oiticica, and others, he was one of the founders of the neoconcrete movement, and author of the "Neoconcrete Manifesto" (1959). Gullar spent several years living in exile in Argentina during the Brazilian dictatorship, returning to his homeland in 1977. Sometime writing critic of the *Jornal do Brasil*, he continued to publish prolifically until his death, awarded the Camões Prize for Literature (2010), and Prêmio Jabuti Book of the Year (2011). In 2009, he was included in *Época* magazine's list of the 100 most influential Brazilians and on October 9, 2014, Gullar was elected to membership of the Brazilian Academy of Letters.

Paula Pape is the daughter of the artist Lygia Pape, with whom she created Projeto Lygia Pape in Rio de Janeiro. A photographer and journalist, in addition to personal projects her work has been published in magazines including *Desfile*, *Manchete*, and *Vogue Brasil*; she has shot campaigns for Coca-Cola and Piraquê. Paula is also a law graduate specializing in copyright. She began working with her mother in 1982, rephotographing the collection of works and together organizing the catalogue raisonné. Formally established in 2004, Projeto Lygia Pape still operates within the parameters set by the artist.

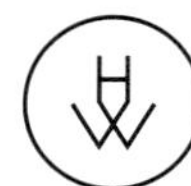

Lygia Pape
September 6–October 20, 2018
Hauser & Wirth New York

Exhibition
Concept:
Projeto Lygia Pape with
Olivier Renaud-Clément

Project assistance:
Pedro Pape Fortes, António Leal,
Astrid Suzano, Projeto Lygia Pape;
Susie Guzman, Catherine Serrano,
Hauser & Wirth

Publication
Concept:
Olivier Renaud-Clément

Design and typesetting:
Damien Saatdjian

Copy editing and proofreading:
Tamsin Perrett

Color separations:
LUP AG, Cologne

Printed by DZA Druckerei zu
Altenburg, Germany

Cover Material: Brillianta 4004
Endpapers: Colorplan Bright Red,
120g/qm
Paper: Tatami White, 150 g/qm
Typeface: Plain (Optimo)

Texts © 2018 the authors

Published by:
Hauser & Wirth Publishers
www.hauserwirth.com

Projeto Lygia Pape
www.lygiapape.com

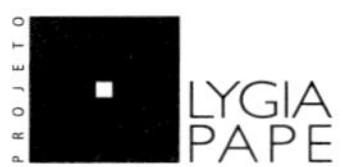

Library of Congress Cataloging-in-
Publication Data is available upon
request.

ISBN: 978-3-906915-14-2

Printed and bound in Germany

Photography Credits
pp. 4, 11, 18: Paula Pape; pp. 10,
13, 14, 20, 21, 27, 29, 31, 33, 35–37,
39, 41–43, 45–47, 49, 51, 53, 55, 57,
59, 61, 63, 64, 67–81, 84, 85, 88–102,
111–29: Genevieve Hanson; pp.
19, 82, 83, 86, 87, 133–37: Timothy
Doyon; p. 22: Ken Adlard; p. 131:
Julio Roriz.

Frontispiece (p. 4): Lygia Pape
with *Amazonino Vermelho e Preto*
(Red and Black Amazonino), 1990.

All works by Lygia Pape © 2018
Projeto Lygia Pape; courtesy Projeto
Lygia Pape and Hauser & Wirth.

Every effort has been made
to trace copyright ownership
and to obtain reproduction
permissions. Corrections brought
to the publisher's attention will be
incorporated in future reprints or
editions of this book.